A Practitioner's G
Investment

Whilst every care has been taken to ensure the accuracy of the contents of this work, no responsibility for loss occasioned to any person acting or refraining from action as a result of any statement in it can be accepted by the authors or the publishers.

A Practitioner's Guide to Trustee Investment

Michael O'Sullivan MA (Cantab), BCL (Oxon), TEP
Barrister, 5 Stone Buildings, Lincoln's Inn
Tom Entwistle BA (Oxon)
Barrister, 5 Stone Buildings, Lincoln's Inn

Members of the LexisNexis Group worldwide

United Kingdom	LexisNexis UK, a Division of Reed Elsevier (UK) Ltd, Halsbury House, 35 Chancery Lane, LONDON WC2A 1EL, and 4 Hill Street, EDINBURGH EH2 3JZ
Argentina	LexisNexis Argentina, BUENOS AIRES
Australia	LexisNexis Butterworths, CHATSWOOD, New South Wales
Austria	LexisNexis Verlag ARD Orac GmbH & Co KG, VIENNA
Canada	LexisNexis Butterworths, MARKHAM, Ontario
Chile	LexisNexis Chile Ltda, SANTIAGO DE CHILE
Czech Republic	Nakladatelství Orac sro, PRAGUE
France	Editions du Juris-Classeur SA, PARIS
Germany	LexisNexis Deutschland GmbH, FRANKFURT and MUNSTER
Hong Kong	LexisNexis Butterworths, HONG KONG
Hungary	HVG-Orac, BUDAPEST
India	LexisNexis Butterworths, NEW DELHI
Ireland	LexisNexis, DUBLIN
Italy	Giuffrè Editore, MILAN
Malaysia	Malayan Law Journal Sdn Bhd, KUALA LUMPUR
New Zealand	LexisNexis Butterworths, WELLINGTON
Poland	Wydawnictwo Prawnicze LexisNexis, WARSAW
Singapore	LexisNexis Butterworths, SINGAPORE
South Africa	LexisNexis Butterworths, DURBAN
Switzerland	Stämpfli Verlag AG, BERNE
USA	LexisNexis, DAYTON, Ohio

First published in 2003

© Reed Elsevier (UK) Ltd 2003

A CIP Catalogue record for this book is available from the British Library.

ISBN 0 40696 528 5

Typeset by Kerrypress Ltd, Luton, Bedfordshire

Printed and bound in Great Britain by The Cromwell Press Limited, Trowbridge, Wiltshire

Visit LexisNexis UK at www.lexisnexis.co.uk

Preface

On 1 February 2001 the Trustee Act 2000 came into force. This Act, which was the product of much hard work by the Law Commission, made sweeping changes to the law relating to trustee investment. Out went the old list-based system of the Trustee Investments Act 1961 and in came a new wide power of investment hedged around by safeguards. Trustees exercising powers of investment are subject to a new statutory duty of care. They are required to take appropriate advice and to have regard to the 'standard investment criteria'. The days of trustees being able to invest a trust fund and sit back and forget about it for years have well and truly gone. The new regime imposes new demands on trustees and in our ever more litigious society trustees need to be aware of what is expected of them if they are to avoid claims for breach of duty. This book aims to provide a guide to the new law. As, to date, little illumination on the new Act has been provided by the courts, the new law is contrasted with the old law and examined against the background of the cases that were decided under the old law.

We would like to thank the staff at LexisNexis UK for their unfailing courtesy and patience. We would also like to thank Toby Harris for allowing the reproduction of a specimen policy statement created by him and our colleague in chambers Penny Reed who allowed us access to the collection of useful materials that she has gathered on the subject of the new Act.

Michael O'Sullivan and Tom Entwistle
5 Stone Buildings, Lincoln's Inn

Contents

Table of Cases

Table of Statutes

References in the right-hand column are to paragraph number. Paragraph references printed in **bold** type indicate where the Act is set out in part or in full.

Table of Statutory Instruments

Chapter 1

Introduction

Background

1.1　　The Trustee Act 2000, which received the Royal Assent on 23 November 2000 and which came into force on 1 February 2001, dramatically changed the law in relation to trustee investment. The Act provides a very wide general power of investment and it will therefore be the starting point for any trustee. The power applies to trusts whenever they were created and so applies to existing trusts as well as new ones created after February 2001. The Act was the brainchild of the Law Commission which had made numerous recommendations for change in its report, 'Trustees' Powers and Duties' (1999) (Law Com no 260, Scot Law Com no 172).

Prior to the Trustee Act 2000, trustee investment was governed by the Trustee Investments Act 1961. That Act provided for division of the trust fund into two parts, known as the narrow range and wider range parts. The narrow range part of the fund had to be invested in narrow range investments as listed in the Act. The wider range part was available for investment in narrow range or wider range investments. Narrow range investments were essentially mortgages of land and a range of gilts and bonds. Wider range investment included equities in the United Kingdom and, since 1994, most European countries. The 1961 Act was therefore list based. In other words, it provided a list of permitted types of investment.

Limitations of the old law

1.2　　The 1999 Law Commission Report noted that trust law was of wider application than was commonly appreciated. Trusts were not confined to the Dickensian world of wills and family settlements. They were relevant to many commercial enterprises from international financial transactions to the management of pension and other investment funds. In the view of the Law Commission, the law governing trustees' powers and duties had not kept pace with the evolving economic and social nature of trusts. The default powers which trustees had under the old law were generally regarded as seriously restrictive (see Law Com no 260, para 1.1). Indeed previously, the Law Reform Committee in 1982 had described the Trustee Investments Act 1961 in stronger terms as 'tiresome, cumbrous and expensive in operation with the result that its provisions are now seen to be inadequate'.

It was true that many trusts contained express powers that enabled trustees to invest in a wide choice of investment products, but there were many older trusts that did not contain such powers and which were governed by the 1961 Act. Further, the 1961 Act applied to home-made wills and trusts and to intestacies.

Principal changes

1.3   A number of fundamental changes in the way investment business was transacted in the 1990s brought into sharp focus the limitations of the old law. The principal changes were:

- the introduction in 1995 of a five-day rolling settlement for dealings in shares and securities listed on the London Stock Exchange;

- the introduction in 1996 of the CREST system which involved the paperless holding of, and transfer of title to, shares and securities listed on the London Stock Exchange;

- the use of similar computerised systems in other markets in which trustees might wish to invest;

- the widespread employment of discretionary fund managers to enable full advantage to be taken of an increasingly complex range of investment opportunities.

It was not just the Trustee Investments Act 1961 that was the problem. The rules which governed collective delegation of trustees' fiduciary discretions were also unduly restrictive and often forced trustees to commit breaches of trust in order to achieve the most effective administration of the trust. Further, trustees in England and Wales did not have adequate statutory powers to enable them to employ nominees and custodians in connection with a range of modern investment services. It was clear that it would not be enough to simply reform the Trustee Investments Act 1961 without tackling the law relating to delegation and the use of nominees and custodians, since the practice of modern investment management meant that trustee investment was inextricably linked with the use of agents and nominees if a trust was to achieve optimum investment performance.

Law Commission recommendations

1.4   To address the perceived problems the Law Commission recommended that:

(*a*)   the Trustee Investments Act 1961 should be replaced with a new statutory provision giving trustees power to make an investment of any kind as if they were absolutely (or beneficially) entitled to the assets of the trust;

(*b*)   trustees should have power to acquire land on behalf of the trust;

(*c*)   trustees should have power to delegate to agents their administrative powers (other than powers to appoint or dismiss trustees) including their power of investment and management but should not have power to delegate their distributive powers over capital or income;

(*d*)   trustees should have power to vest assets in the names of a nominee and to deposit documents or trust property with a custodian for safe keeping;

(*e*)   all trustees should have power to insure the trust property as they would if they were the absolute owners of it;

(*f*)   trustees should have power to authorise one or more of their number to charge for his or her services on behalf of the trust if he or she was acting in a professional capacity;

(*g*)   trustees should be subject to a general duty of care requiring them to act with such care and skill as was reasonable in the circumstances, having regard in particular to any special knowledge or experience that he or she had or held himself or herself out as having and if he or she acts as a trustee in the course of a business or profession, to any special knowledge that it was reasonable to expect of a person acting in the course of that kind of business or profession.

The recommendations were substantially enacted and little, if any, damage was done to the Law Commission proposals in the course of the Trustee Bill's passage through Parliament.

The general power of investment in the Trustee Act 2000 and the other relevant provisions of the Act are considered in more detail in the chapters that follow. However, before that, it is proposed to consider some fundamental issues.

The meaning of investment

1.5   The term 'investment' is not defined in the Trustee Act 2000. Commentators have criticised this omission. However, the failure to provide a definition was no doubt deliberate. Probably, the Law Commission felt that a detailed statutory definition might prove insufficiently flexible to catch every kind of product now in existence or which might be dreamt up in the future and one that was in general terms would be of little assistance to defining an ordinary everyday concept.

Interpretation

1.6   In the case of *IRC v Desoutter Bros Ltd [1946] 1 All ER 58*, Lord Greene MR stated that the term 'investment' was not a term of art but had to be interpreted in a popular sense. The case concerned the question whether the profits derived from the exploitation of patents by a manufacturing company was income from investments for the purposes of the Finance (No 2) Act 1939, Sch 7, Part I. The Master of the Rolls, in referring to attempts by counsel on both sides to define the term, said at page 60:

> 'The question whether or not a particular piece of income is received from an investment must, in my view, be decided upon the facts of the case. The facts must be ascertained and then the question has to be answered. For the court to find itself fettered by some apparently comprehensive attempt at a definition directed to the solution of the problem in relation to one type of property, I cannot help thinking is unfortunate. It may well be that a definition or test, when applied to one type of property, is a useful method of approaching the particular problem in the particular case, but to take it as a guide in other cases is apt to be extremely dangerous and certainly in the present case I do not propose to do so.'

In a trust context, *Re Wragg [1919] 2 Ch 58* considered whether trustees of a will had power to appropriate real property in satisfaction of the beneficiaries' interests. This turned on whether the trustees had power to invest in real property. In holding that the widely drawn power of investment in the particular will did provide such power, PO Lawrence J said:

> 'Without attempting to give an exhaustive definition of the words "invest" and "investment", I think that the verb "to invest" when used in an investment clause may safely be said to include as one of its meanings "to apply money in the purchase of some property from which interest or profit is expected and which property is purchased in order to be held for the sake of the income which it will yield"; whilst the noun "investment" when used in such a clause may safely be said to include as one of its meanings "the property in the purchase of which the money has been so applied" '.

According to this definition, something will not qualify as an investment unless it is expected to produce an income or profit. On this basis, it was held that trustees with a power to invest in freehold property could not validly exercise the power to acquire property for the occupation of beneficiaries (*Re Power [1947] 2 All ER 282*). This was because such a purchase might not be a purchase by way of investment in as much as part of the money would, or might be, paid for the advantage of vacant possession and the benefit which the beneficiaries would get by living in the house.

The judge in *Re Wragg* was at pains to make clear that his attempted definition was not exhaustive and nowadays it should not be a necessary requirement of an investment that it must produce an income. It should be sufficient that the investment generates a capital return. Certainly, in the case of *Harries v Church Commissioners for England [1993] 2 All ER 300*, Sir Donald Nicholls V-C, in considering the extent to which the Church Commissioners were entitled to take into account non-financial ethical considerations when investing the funds under their control, drew a distinction between property held by a charity for functional purposes and property held as an investment. This latter property he described as:

'property held by the trustees for the purposes of generating money whether from income or capital'.

The explanatory notes to the Trustee Bill are consistent with the contention that an investment can be capital growth generating rather than income producing. Those notes stated:

'"Investment" is not defined in the Bill. The general power permits the trustees to invest assets in a way which is expected to produce an income or a capital return'.

In the absence of any statutory definition of the term 'investment', one ought to be entitled to have regard to the ordinary meaning of the word as currently understood. The essence of the concept is that it is something that is acquired in order to produce a return rather than for another purpose.

The meaning of trust and trustee

1.7   The Trustee Act 2000 does not define 'trustee' or 'trust'. The explanatory notes to the Trustee Bill in the glossary of terms at Annex A define 'trustee' in the following terms:

'A trustee is a person who has property or rights (trust property or assets) which he holds or is bound to exercise for or on behalf of another or others, or for the accomplishment of some particular purpose or purposes. He or she is said to hold the property on trust for that other or others, or for that purpose'.

Other similar definitions can be found in leading textbooks on trust law – see Underhill and Hayton, *The Law Relating to Trusts and Trustees* (16th edn, 2003) LexisNexis UK (at p 3), Lewin, *Lewin on Trusts* (17th edn) Sweet & Maxwell (Ch 1, paras 1.01–1.04). Article 2 of the Convention on the Law Applicable to Trusts and on Their Recognition defines a trust in the following terms:

'. . . the term "trust" refers to the legal relationship created – inter vivos or on death – by a person, the settlor, when assets have been placed under the control of a trustee for the benefit of a beneficiary or for a specified purpose'.

Characteristics of a trust

1.8   A trust has the following characteristics:

* the assets constitute a separate fund and are not part of the trustee's own estate;

- title to the trust assets stands in the name of the trustee or in the name of another person on behalf of the trustee;

- the trustee has the power and the duty, in respect of which he is accountable, to manage, employ or dispose of the assets in accordance with the terms of the trust and the special duties imposed upon him by law.

The reservation by the settlor of certain rights and powers, and the fact that the trustee may himself have rights as a beneficiary, are not necessarily inconsistent with the existence of a trust.

Constructive/bare trusts

1.9   The question arises as to whether the Act applies to constructive trusts and bare trusts as well as to express trusts. In the absence of any statutory definition, and applying the definitions referred to above, the answer ought to be yes. This is possibly a sterile question as far as constructive trusts are concerned because such trusts are often imposed over specific property as a form of remedy, and so questions of investment of the trust property do not generally arise. In the same way, bare trusts – where property is held for another absolutely – do not usually involve questions of trustee investment because the property is held on bare trust for a purpose, eg as part of a commercial transaction, and the beneficial owner can always direct the trustee how to deal with the property. Investment of the fund is seldom going to be an issue that exercises either trustee or beneficiary. Section 34 of the Trustee Act 2000, which deals with the power to insure, makes it clear that that section applies to bare trustees. This section expressly states that the power to insure in the case of a bare trust is subject to any direction given by the beneficiary. One would think that if the other provisions were intended to apply to bare trusts the Act would make it clear that the other powers conferred, eg the power of investment, were also subject to the beneficiary's direction. The fact that the duty to insure applies to bare trusts suggests that the duty of investment also applies (see *Lewin on Trusts* at para 34–01J). It remains to be seen whether this question proves to be a real issue requiring the court to shed light on it.

Personal representatives

1.10   The Trustee Act 2000 clearly applies to personal representatives administering an estate. This is made plain by section 35 of the Trustee Act 2000 which goes on to provide that for this purpose the Act is to be read with the appropriate modifications listed in subsection (2).

The duty to invest

1.11   Trustees have a duty to invest the trust fund in their hands. Property must be acquired or retained in order to produce a financial return for the trust:

Robinson v Robinson (1851) 1 De GM & G 247, 42 ER 547; Stafford v Fiddon (1857) 23 Beav 386, 53 ER 151. A failure to invest the trust fund will expose the trustee to a claim for breach of trust.

Other duties

1.12   In exercising powers of investment, trustees are obliged to have regard to certain other general principles of trust law. It is a paramount duty of trustees to exercise their powers in the best interests of the present and future beneficiaries of the trust (*Cowan v Scargill [1985] Ch 270, 286–287*). They are also subject to the duty not to profit from their office or to cause loss to the trust as a result of conflict between their fiduciary duty and self interest. They have a duty to comply with the terms of the trust and to act impartially between the beneficiaries. They have particular obligations in relation to dealings with trust property as between a tenant for life and a remainderman and as to the treatment of income and capital generally.

Chapter 2

The Statutory Power of Investment under the Trustee Act 2000

Introduction

2.1   Section 3(1) of the Trustee Act 2000 provides that subject to the provisions of Part II of the Act, a trustee 'may make any kind of investment that he could make if he were absolutely entitled to the assets of the trust'.

This power is referred to in the Act as the 'general power of investment'. The words used in the section differ from the wording used in most modern trusts. For example, the standard provisions of the Society of Trust and Estate Practitioners use the words: 'the Trustees may invest Trust Property in any manner as if they were beneficial owners . . .'

In the majority of cases the distinction between the statutory wording and the 'beneficial owner' form of wording will make no material difference. However, the statutory wording does import a personal element which makes its effect turn on what the trustee is able to do with assets that he owns absolutely. This might limit the powers of a corporate trustee that is subject to limitations under its own constitution.

Section 3(2) of the Act states that the general power of investment does not permit a trustee to make investments in land other than loans secured on land. This is a limitation that does not usually appear in modern express trustee investment clauses. Section 8 of the Trustee Act 2000, however, provides a power to acquire land as an investment and for other purposes. The term 'loan secured on land' is explained in section 3(4). A person invests in a loan secured on land if he has rights under any contract under which one person provides another with credit, and the obligation of the borrower to repay is secured on land. 'Credit' is defined as including any cash loan or other financial accommodation. Cash includes money in any form.

Restriction and exclusion

2.2   Section 6 of the Trustee Act 2000 provides that the general power is in addition to powers conferred on trustees other than by the Act but is subject to any restriction or exclusion imposed by the trust instrument or any enactment or by any provision of subordinate legislation. For the purposes of the Act, an enactment or provision of subordinate legislation is not to be regarded as being part of a trust instrument. 'Subordinate legislation' has the same meaning as in the Interpretation Act 1978 – see section 6(3) of the Trustee Act 2000. It therefore means Orders in Council, orders, rules, regulations, schemes, warrants, by-laws and other instruments made or to be made under any Act, including any local, personal or private Act.

A restriction in an instrument will need to be a clear restriction if it is to limit the new general power of investment in the Act. It is thought that the grant of a limited power of investment will not oust the more general statutory power but an express prohibition against a particular type of investment will. Thus, being authorised to invest in the shares of banks and insurance companies would not oust the power to invest more widely but if it was expressed as a power to invest only in shares of banks or insurance companies, the statutory power would be ousted. That was the position under the Trustee Investments Act 1961 and its predecessors. However, section 1(3) of the 1961 Act used different wording from that in section 6(1) of the Trustee Act 2000. The wording in the 1961 Act was ' .... those powers are exercisable only so far as a contrary intention is not expressed in any Act or instrument . . .'.

In *Re Warren [1939] Ch 684*, the court held that the same form of words in the earlier section 69(2) of the Trustee Act 1925 meant the same as the words 'a trustee may, unless expressly forbidden by the instrument .' used in section 1 of the Trustee Act 1893.

Simonds J reached his decision on the grounds that the 1925 Act was a consolidating statute and should not therefore have altered the law on the relevant point. In *Re Burke [1908] 2 Ch 248*, which was a decision under section 1 of the 1893 Act, it was held that a direction in a will to invest the fund on a specified deposit account at a bank did not preclude the trustees from investing in other securities authorised under the 1893 Act because the direction did not amount to an express prohibition. The argument that the direction inferentially forbade the investment of the fund in other ways was rejected. The 1893 Act was held to mean what it said. While probably the same approach would be taken under the Trustee Act 2000 and a clear limitation or exclusion would be required, the statutory wording used:

'The general power of investment is—

(a)   in addition to powers conferred on trustees otherwise than by this Act, but

(b)   subject to any restriction or exclusion imposed by the trust instrument or by any enactment or any provision of subordinate legislation',

will probably leave scope for more argument that implied restrictions are present on the wording of particular instruments, particularly where a settlor or testator positively directs that the fund shall be invested in a particular way but does not use words that expressly prohibit investment in any other way.

In the Law Commission's report that led up to the 2000 Act, the notes to the draft Bill said that clause 6, which was in the same terms as the enacted section 6, made it clear that:

> 'those trustees who benefit from limited express powers of investment will also have the general power of investment under clause 3 unless that power is expressly or *impliedly* excluded' [emphasis added].

The view expressed in *Lewin on Trusts* (at 35–01D n 13), that the same result as was arrived at in *Re Burke* would follow on the words of the Trustee Act 2000, may need to be treated with a degree of caution.

Appointments under pre-1961 settlements

2.3   Section 7(2) of the Trustee Act 2000 provides that no provision relating to the powers of a trustee contained in a trust instrument made before 3 August 1961 is to be treated (for the purposes of section 6(1)(b)) as restricting or excluding the general power of investment. This provision was intended to ensure that any old restrictions which the Trustee Investments Act 1961 removed do not revive.

It is unclear what the position is when an appointment containing restrictions on investment is made on or after 3 August 1961 under a special power of appointment created by a settlement or will made before that date. *Lewin on Trusts* suggests that the better view is that such an appointment will be capable of taking effect as a trust instrument made on or after 3 August 1961. However, if the appointment merely applies the restrictive powers contained in the original will or settlement, the restrictions will be taken as being contained in the will or settlement and not in the appointment, even if the power of appointment was wide enough to authorise changes in the investment powers. The point turns on the meaning of 'trust instrument' as used in section 6(1)(b). The general definition section, section 39(2), provides no general definition of the term but does make reference to sections 6(2) and 35(2)(a). Section 6(2) provides that an enactment or provision of subordinate legislation is not to be regarded as being or as being part of a trust instrument. Section 35 is concerned with the Act's application to personal representatives and subsection (2)(a) provides that references to the trust instrument are to be read as references to the will. These provisions therefore provide little illumination on the power of appointment question.

In other contexts, a reference to the date of the instrument is taken as being a reference to the date of the appointment, not the date of the instrument creating the power. For example, section 31 of the Trustee Act 1925 applies to an appointment made after 1 January 1926 under a special power conferred by a pre-1926 instrument (*Re Dickinson's Settlements [1939] Ch 27*; *Re De la Bere's Marriage Settlement Trusts [1941] Ch 443*). In the same way, where a post-

1969 appointment is made in exercise of a special power conferred by a pre-1970 instrument, Part I of the Family Law Reform Act 1969 applies to reduce the age of majority to 18 (*Begg-MacBrearty v Stilwell [1996] 4 All ER 205*). Applying a similar approach, the words 'trust instrument' should be construed in the same way as the word 'instrument' has been construed in the above contexts and the appointment itself should be the relevant instrument.

Applicability to pre-2000 instruments

2.4   Part II of the Trustee Act 2000 is stated in section 7 to apply to trusts whether created before or after the commencement of the Act. No provision relating to the powers of a trustee contained in a trust instrument made before 3 August 1961 is to be treated for the purposes of section 6(1)(b) as restricting or excluding the general power of investment. The said date is the date when the Trustee Investments Act 1961 came into force. Only exclusions or restrictions contained in instruments after this date will cut down the general power of investment. Therefore, old restrictions that were superseded by the Trustee Investments Act 1961 cannot revive and restrict the new general power in the 2000 Act. Section 7(3) is intended to ensure that express powers of investment which operate by reference to the powers conferred on trustees by the Trustee Investments Act 1961 will, in future, be treated as conferring the general power of investment.

Non-application of general power to certain specific cases

2.5   The general power of investment is not available to trustees of pension funds – see section 36(3) Trustee Act 2000; authorised unit trusts – see section 37(1) Trustee Act 2000; or certain charity funds – section 38 Trustee Act 2000.

Safeguards

2.6   The Law Commission considered that the creation of the new general investment power needed to be balanced by the imposition of safeguards. As a result, Part II of the Act contains two safety mechanisms:

- a duty to consider the suitability of investments and the need for diversification of investments, ie the standard investment criteria in section 4 of the Trustee Act 2000;

- a duty to take proper advice (section 5 of the Trustee Act 2000).

These safeguards are concerned with the exercise of the power of investment rather than the scope of such power. They are also applicable to the exercise of any power of investment and not just the general statutory power. For this reason they are considered in CHAPTER 4: EXERCISE OF POWERS OF INVESTMENT.

Chapter 3

Express Powers of Investment

Construing the meaning

3.1   The scope of an express investment power is a matter of construction of its wording. Trusts are construed according to well-established principles of construction. The court seeks to ascertain the meaning of a settlement or a will from the words used by the settlor or testator. The court applies the ordinary meaning of ordinary words. Technical words are given their technical meaning. The court is entitled to have regard to the surrounding circumstances or the matrix of facts in interpreting the document. Direct evidence of the subjective intention of a settlor is not, however, admissible in the case of a lifetime trust. In the case of wills, where a testator dies after 31 December 1982, evidence of the testator's subjective intention is admissible under section 21 of the Administration of Justice Act 1982 in so far as part of a will is meaningless or ambiguous on the face of the document or external evidence shows that the language used in any part of the will is ambiguous in the light of surrounding circumstances. The court has regard to the instrument as a whole in order to construe the meaning of part of it.

Analysis of wording

3.2   The importance of correctly analysing the wording of an investment clause can be seen in the following two examples.

In *R v Barlow Clowes (No 2) [1994] 2 All ER 316* the directors of the Barlow Clowes group of companies were tried for theft and other offences of dishonesty. The Barlow Clowes group of companies had marketed an investment scheme for offshore investment in gilts. Funds invested had not been invested in gilts but had been placed in deposit accounts and withdrawn by Mr Clowes for his own personal use. As part of their defence, the directors sought to argue that the relationship between investors and Barlow Clowes was not one of trustee and beneficiary but rather that of debtor and creditor. They also sought to rely on a clause in the scheme documentation that stated that the company was authorised:

> 'to place any uninvested funds with any bank, local authority, corporation or other body on such terms and conditions as you see fit whether bearing interest or not'.

The Court of Appeal held that the relationship was one of trustee and beneficiary and construed that the above clause was merely ancillary to the use of the
funds to invest in gilts and that it did not justify the use that had actually been
made of the funds by providing a wide general discretionary power of investment. In *Nestle v National Westminster Bank plc [1993] 1 WLR 1260*, the
relevant investment clause gave the trustee power to invest in:

> 'any securities or investments of the same or a similar nature to any
> belonging to the testator at the time of his death or in the stock shares
> bonds debentures or securities of any railway or other company'.

The bank, without taking legal advice, regarded that clause as limiting its power
to invest the trust funds in ordinary shares. It thought it could only invest in
ordinary shares in companies in which the testator at death had a holding or in
similar companies. After the Trustee Investments Act 1961 came into force it
regarded its powers as wholly governed by that Act. In fact, the clause gave it
power to invest in the stocks and shares of any company. The bank was sued for
breach of trust and the Court of Appeal upheld Hoffmann J's decision that it had
misconstrued its power.

Modern construction of investment powers

3.3   Traditionally, investment powers were construed strictly by the courts.
In *Bethell v Abraham (1873) LR 17 Eq 24,* the relevant clause was in the
following terms:

> 'All the residue of the income of my estate shall be accumulated and
> invested at the discretion of my trustees ... and the moneys also
> receivable on my policies shall be invested at their discretion. My trustees
> shall not be obliged to alter any investment or to convert perishable into
> permanent securities, but may continue or change securities from time to
> time as [*sic*] the majority shall seem meet'.

Sir George Jessel MR rejected the contention that this clause conferred on the
trustees an absolute discretion as to the investments to be made. He held that the
discretionary words could refer to the time of investment or the question
whether an investment should be changed or not. It is unlikely that the same
clause would be so restrictively interpreted by a modern court in the era of the
Trustee Act 2000.

In *Re Maryon-Wilson's Estate [1912] 1 Ch 55*, the Court of Appeal had to
consider whether a power to invest in the stocks or securities of any British
colony or dependency allowed trustees to invest in the stocks of any province of
the Dominion of Canada. In holding that the trustees could not invest in the
stocks of any province unless that province had complied with the requirements
of the Colonial Stock Act 1900, Cozens-Hardy MR said:

> 'A clause of this nature enlarging the power of investment beyond what the
> general law sanctions, ought, I think, to be construed strictly. It is for those

who seek to include a particular investment to prove beyond all reasonable doubt that the words of the clause cover it'.

Farwell LJ was of the same mind, stating:

'. . . if a greater latitude is to be allowed, testators and settlors should express its extent in clear terms'.

This approach was, however, softened a little in the case of *Re Peczenik's Settlement Trusts [1964] 1 WLR 720*. There a settlor directed that her trustee should stand possessed of the trust fund for the purpose of investing such funds in any shares stocks property or property holding company as the trustees in their discretion shall consider to be in the best interests of [S]. Buckley J held that although investment clauses ought to be construed strictly, the meaning of the language should not be restricted unduly and that on the true construction of this settlement, the trustees were authorised to invest in any shares, stock or property being property capable of being treated as an investment. They were not, however, authorised to invest merely upon personal security.

It is considered that in a modern document a power to invest in such manner as the trustees think fit will normally cover anything that can properly be called an investment. If the clause in addition says that the trustees have all the powers of a beneficial owner, then this puts the matter beyond doubt.

Personal security

3.4   In the absence of a clear direction trustees, even when they have a discretion, cannot lend trust funds on the security of a personal promise, however trustworthy the borrower appears to be – *Holmes v Dring (1788) 2 Cox Eq Cas 1*. In that case, Lord Kenyon said that this principle 'ought to be rung into the ears of everyone who acts in the character of a trustee'.

In the case of *Khoo Tek Keong v Ch'ng Joo Twan Neoh [1934] AC 529*, the Privy Council held that a power given to trustees to invest moneys in such investments as they in their absolute discretion thought fit, did not authorise them to lend it at interest upon a mere personal agreement to repay.

A power to lend on personal security may, depending upon the construction of the relevant power, be construed as a power to lend on the security of personal property rather than on a mere promise to repay. For example, where the expression 'personal security' is juxtaposed with the expression 'real security', the correct construction is probably restricted to security on personal property – see Underhill and Hayton, 15th edn (p 595), commenting on *Pickard v Anderson (1872) LR 13 Eq 608*. A power to invest on 'personal credit without security' was held to permit trustees to lend without security in *Re Laing's Settlement [1899] 1 Ch 593*. In that case, it was also held that trustees who had power with the consent of the life tenant to lend on personal security were not precluded from lending to the life tenant himself. If, however, joint trustees have power to lend on personal security, they may not lend to one of themselves (*Anton v Walker (1828) 5 Russ 7*). Even if trustees have a power to lend on a personal obligation they must only exercise the power in good faith and do so for the benefit of the trust. They must not exercise the power simply to accommodate the borrower (*Langston v Ollivant (1807) Coop G 33*).

Investment in companies

3.5   A power to invest in the shares or securities of a 'company incorporated by an Act of Parliament' does not authorise an investment in securities of a company which is only incorporated under the Companies Acts (*Re Smith [1896] 2 Ch 590*). A power to invest in the securities of any 'railway or other public company' was held to include the securities of companies under the Companies Act and since such companies were incorporated under the authority of a public statute, the instruments forming their constitution were accessible to the public and their shares were transferable to members of the public (*Re Sharp (1890) 45 Ch D 286*). A power to invest in 'any of the public funds or in government or real or leasehold securities or upon the stocks shares or securities of any railway or other public company' was held in *Re Castlehow [1903] 1 Ch 352* to be restricted to public companies in the United Kingdom and not to authorise retention of shares in an American steamship company which had been substituted for English steamship company shares under a scheme of amalgamation. Byrne J reached this decision by reading the words 'other public company' in connection with the preceding words of the clause.

Businesses outside the UK

3.6   In *Re Hilton [1909] 2 Ch 548* it was held that a direction permitting investment in companies in the United Kingdom permitted investment in companies registered in the United Kingdom but carrying on business abroad. Where a power to invest was a power to invest in the stocks, funds or securities of 'any corporation or company, municipal, commercial or otherwise' it was held that the trustees had power to invest in the stocks, funds or securities of companies, incorporated and unincorporated, formed or registered within the United Kingdom but carrying on business abroad, and also of companies formed or registered outside the United Kingdom (*Re Stanley [1906] 1 Ch 131*).

'Blue chip category'

3.7   A direction to invest in stocks 'in the blue chip category' was held void for uncertainty in *Re Kolb's Will Trusts [1962] Ch 531*. Whether this decision would be followed today is perhaps questionable. In *Re Gulbenkian's Settlement Trusts (Whishaw v Stephens [1970] AC 508)* the House of Lords said a power of appointment was valid even though a comprehensive list of its objects could not be drawn up. It was enough that it was possible to say with certainty of any given postulant that he definitely was or was not an object of the power. In a similar way, it should be possible to tell whether a given stock is of blue chip character or not and so a similar approach might be justified to an investment power as to the scope of a power of appointment.

Foreign bonds

3.8   Stock of the United States of America and even bonds and debentures of the particular states come under the description of 'foreign bonds'. However, bonds or debentures of municipal towns or railway companies abroad are not within the description of foreign bonds (*Ellis v Eden (1857) 23 Beav 543; Re Langdale Settlement Trusts (1870) LR 10 Eq 39*). However, a power to invest 'upon any of the stocks or funds of the Government of the United States of America or of the Government of France or any other foreign government' was held to allow trustees to invest in New York and Ohio stocks and Georgia bonds (*Cadett v Earle (1877) 5 Ch D 710*).

Chapter 4

Exercise of Powers of Investment

The standard investment criteria

4.1   Section 4(1) of the Trustee Act 2000 provides that in exercising any power of investment, whether arising under this Part or otherwise, a trustee must have regard to the standard investment criteria. Section 4(2) provides that a trustee must, from time to time, review the investments of the trust and consider whether, having regard to the standard investment criteria, they should be varied. The standard investment criteria in relation to a trust are defined in section 4(3) as:

- the suitability to the trust of investments of the same kind as any particular investment proposed to be made or retained and of that particular investment as an investment of that kind; and

- the need for diversification of investments of the trust, in so far as is appropriate to the circumstances of the trust.

Section 4 is based on section 6(1) of the Trustee Investments Act 1961 which used similar wording and which applied to both the exercise of the statutory power under the 1961 Act and any express power. Section 4 does not therefore impose any new requirement on trustees. Indeed, section 6(1) of the 1961 Act did not itself change the law but rather put the existing law into statutory form.

The modern theory

4.2   Trustees have to consider the whole range of types of investments open to them. It is not enough for them to consider whether a particular investment is suitable. In considering a particular investment they have to consider the alternative investments available and whether and how the particular investment fits into the portfolio as a whole. Modern portfolio theory emphasises that investments are best managed by balancing risk and return across the whole portfolio rather than looking at each investment in isolation. Section 4(3) is in accord with this modern theory. The applicability of modern portfolio theory to trustee investment was endorsed by Hoffmann J in *Nestle v National Westminster Bank plc*. In (1996) 10 *Trust Law International* he said:

'Modern trustees acting within their investment powers are entitled to be judged by the standards of current portfolio theory, which emphasises the risk level of the entire portfolio rather than the risk attaching to each investment taken in isolation'.

Lord Nicholls in (1995) 9 *Trust Law International* 71 took the same approach:

'Trustee investment policy is aimed at producing a portfolio of investments which is balanced overall and suited to the needs of the particular trust
. . ..

'Such a strategy falls to be judged likewise, that is, overall. Different investments are accompanied by different degrees of risk, which are reflected in the expected rate of return. A large fund with a widely diversified portfolio of securities might justifiably include modest holdings of high risk securities which would be altogether imprudent and out of place in a smaller fund.

'In such a case it would be inappropriate to isolate one particular investment out of a vast portfolio and enquire whether that would be justified as a trust investment. Such "a line-by-line approach" is misplaced. The inquiry, rather, should be to look at a particular investment and enquire whether that is justified as a holding in the context of the overall portfolio. Traditional warnings against the need for trustees to avoid speculative or hazardous investments are not to be read as inhibiting trustees from maintaining a portfolio of investments which contain a prudent and sensible mixture of low risk and higher risk securities. They are not to be so read because they were not directed at a portfolio which is a balanced exercise in risk management.'

The requirement to consider suitability is mandatory whereas diversification is required only if it is appropriate to the circumstances of the trust.

Diversification

4.3   Diversification is not defined in the Act but it is a concept familiar to trustees and fund managers. It means maintaining a spread of investments so that all one's eggs are not in the same basket. Diversification is required in so far as it is appropriate to the needs of the trust. While diversification will be appropriate in most cases, there may be cases where it is appropriate for trustees to maintain the bulk of the fund in one holding, eg the shares in a private family company. In such a case it may be difficult, in practice, to diversify because the provisions of the articles of association of the relevant company may place restrictions on transfer of the shares. This may affect the price which can be achieved.

It will often be perfectly legitimate for trustees to have regard to the wishes of a settlor to keep shares in a private family company within the family. Consideration of the family circumstances and broader family interests of the beneficiaries of a trust is perfectly appropriate provided that the trustees do not act with any ulterior purpose, such as furthering the interests of the settlor himself rather than those of the beneficiaries.

Large funds

4.4   The size of the trust fund will be a factor that affects diversification. In the case of a large fund, diversification will usually be appropriate and indeed necessary – see *Cowan v Scargill [1984] 2 All ER 750*. In that case, Megarry V-C had to consider the Mineworkers Pension Scheme. The trustees appointed by the union refused to approve an annual investment plan for the scheme unless it was amended to prohibit an increase in overseas investment, to provide for withdrawal from overseas investments at an opportune time and to prohibit investment in energy industries that were in competition with coal. The trustees appointed by the National Coal Board applied to the court for directions that the union-appointed trustees were acting in breach of trust by refusing to adopt the proposed investment plan.

Megarry V-C held that the trustees had an overriding duty to do the best they could for the beneficiaries. In considering the need for diversification, which was even more important in the case of a large pension fund, they could not refuse for social or political reasons to make a particular investment if to make that investment would be more beneficial financially to the beneficiaries of the fund.

Other considerations

4.5   Other general considerations that might need to be balanced against the desirability of diversification include the tax position of the trust fund. If the existing investments are pregnant with heavy capital gains it may be unwise to diversify and incur tax changes. Change in the portfolio may need to be managed over a long period of time so that reliefs are used as and when available.

Advice

4.6   Section 5 of the Trustee Act 2000 provides that:

'(1)   Before exercising any power of investment, whether arising under this Part or otherwise, a trustee must (unless the exception applies) obtain and consider proper advice about the way in which, having regard to the standard investment criteria, the power should be exercised.

(2)   When reviewing the investments of the trust, a trustee must (unless

the exception applies) obtain and consider proper advice about whether, having regard to the standard investment criteria, the investments should be varied.

(3)   The exception is that a trustee need not obtain such advice if he reasonably concludes that in all the circumstances it is unnecessary or inappropriate to do so.

(4)   Proper advice is the advice of a person who is reasonably believed by the trustee to be qualified to give it by his ability in and practical experience of financial and other matters relating to the proposed investment.'

Section 5 of the 2000 Act is similar to, and based on, section 6 of the Trustee Investments Act 1961. Section 5, however, applies to the exercise of any investment power and not just the statutory power. A trustee fulfils his duty if he obtains and considers advice. He is not bound to follow such advice and is able to reject it. However, a trustee who makes or changes an investment in the teeth of professional advice will obviously lay himself open to a claim in breach of trust if his decision proves to be ill judged. The statutory duty of care will apply to the taking of and consideration of advice and a trustee will need to have sound reasons for rejecting advice.

The duty to take and consider advice is subject to the exception in subsection (3). There will be some situations in which an investment decision is straightforward, for example where the fund is small and the proposed investment is clearly safe. Further, a trustee himself might be possessed of the necessary financial experience and knowledge to make the decision. In this instance, it would be pointless to require him to obtain advice from a third-party adviser, for a fee, when he was as well placed to advise as that third party. Similarly, a trustee's co-trustee might be qualified to advise the trustee without the need to go to an outside adviser. The decision that the exception applies obviously calls for an exercise of judgement on the part of the trustees. Such a decision should in general be properly minuted.

Written advice

4.7   Section 5 of the Trustee Act 2000 does not require the advice to be given or confirmed in writing. This contrasts with section 6(5) of the Trustee Investments Act 1961 which provided that a trustee was not to be treated as having complied with his statutory duties with regard to taking advice unless the advice was given or confirmed in writing. In practice, trustees will be well advised to obtain written advice or to record the substance of the advice in writing so that they can protect themselves from challenge or criticism later.

The Act does not define precisely who is qualified to give advice. The Treasury consulted on this point and a substantial majority of those who responded on the point thought that the matter should be left to the trustees' discretion (see 2.34 Law Com no 260).

The adviser must be subjectively believed by the trustee to be qualified on objective reasonable grounds so that the choice is one that a reasonable trustee could make in all the circumstances, even if a court might not choose the particular adviser (*Edge v Pensions Ombudsman [2000] Ch 602 at 618–619, 627 and 630*).

The statutory duty of care

4.8   At common law, trustees had a duty when investing to exercise the standard of care that an ordinary prudent man of business would exercise when acting in the management of his own affairs – *Speight v Gaunt (1883) 22 Ch D 727* per Bacon V-C whose statement of the law was endorsed on appeal per Jessel MR: *Re Whiteley (1886) 33 Ch D 347 at 358*.

This standard of prudence required more than just good faith and honesty (*Cowan v Scargill [1985] Ch 270*). A level of competence was, therefore, expected from trustees. However, what level was required varied depending on the facts of the particular case. It was thought that remunerated and professional trustees were expected to meet a higher standard than ordinary lay trustees (*National Trustee Company of Australia v General Finance Co of Australia Ltd [1905] AC 373*; *Re Waterman's Will Trusts [1952] 2 All ER 1054*). A trustee who held himself out as having special expertise beyond that of the ordinary prudent person could be held liable if loss was incurred as a result of failure to exercise that level of expertise (*Bartlett v Barclays Bank (Nos 1 and 2) [1980] Ch 515*). However, this view is not universally accepted – see for example *Lewin on Trusts* at 34–01H which opined that professional trustees and those possessed of special expertise were subject to the same standard of care as non-professionals. This view contrasts with the Law Commission's understanding of the common law position (see paras 2.14 and 2.15 of Law Com no 260).

Law Commission recommendations

4.9   The Law Commission, in its report on 'Trustees' Duties and Powers', felt that the default powers of investment and delegation etc enjoyed by trustees were too limited to enable them to administer trusts in the most effective way in the modern age. As a result, it recommended that new wider statutory powers be conferred. As a counter-balance to this, however, it also recommended that a new uniform statutory duty of care should be imposed. The recommendation that such a duty apply to the exercise of powers of investment was based more on considerations of symmetry rather than on any perceived need to plug a gap in the existing law. The Law Commission stated in its report that the reform which it recommended probably represented no more than a codification of the existing common law duty (see paras 2.35 and 3.16 of Law Com no 260).

Section 1 of the Trustee Act 2000 creates a new statutory duty of care. Section 2 states that Schedule 1 to the Act makes provision about when the duty of care applies to a trustee. Schedule 1, paragraph 1 makes it clear that the duty applies to a trustee when exercising the statutory power of investment or any other power of investment however conferred. The duty of care also applies when a trustee is exercising the ancillary duty imposed by section 4 (ie having regard to the standard investment criteria when making or reviewing investments) and section 5 (ie taking advice before exercising or reviewing investments).

The duty as expressed in section 1(1) is the duty to:

'. . . exercise such care and skill as is reasonable in the circumstances, having regard in particular:

(a)   to any special knowledge or experience that he has or holds himself out as having, and

(b)   if he acts as trustee in the course of a business or profession, to any special knowledge or experience that it is reasonable to expect of a person acting in the course of that kind of business or profession'.

The statutory duty applies to trusts already in existence at the date of the Act's commencement. However, it does not have retrospective effect so that any alleged breaches of duty committed before the Act came into force will need to be judged by the old common law standard. As noted above, it is doubtful whether the new statutory duty of care imposes any higher or different standard than the old test.

Specialist knowledge

4.10   Section 1(1)(a) imposes a subjective standard on any person who holds himself out as having special knowledge or experience. Section 1(1)(b) imposes an objective standard on a professional trustee or paid trustee acting in the course of his business. In practice, in the case of solicitors and accountants and the like, their performance will be probably be judged according to the standards of skill and care expected of their respective professions. However, in an age where professionals market their services more aggressively and overtly than they used to, section 1(1)(a) might expose firms to greater potential liabilities. If a professional claims a very high degree of expertise in trust management, he may live to regret it if he fails to deliver the promised 'Rolls Royce' service. In *Bartlett v Barclays Trust Co (No 2) [1980] Ch 515*, Brightman J obviously attached considerable weight to the claims made in advertising literature:

'A trust corporation holds itself out in its advertising literature as being above ordinary mortals. With a specialist staff of trained trust officers and managers, with ready access to financial information and professional advice, dealing with and solving trust problems day after day, the trust corporation holds itself out and rightly, as capable of providing an expertise which it would be unrealistic to expect and unjust to demand from the ordinary prudent man or woman who accepts, probably unpaid and sometimes reluctantly from a sense of family duty, the burdens of trusteeship'.

Lewin on Trusts at paragraph 34–01H suggests that the converse may apply and that a lay trustee may find it easier to defend a claim for negligence under the new law than under the old common law. In the author's view, while it may be true that a lay trustee who defers to the view of a professional trustee may perhaps be excused more readily, there must be a minimum standard below which a trustee cannot fall, and if the new statutory duty merely codifies the old law, then a lay trustee will still need to satisfy the standard of the ordinary prudent man of business managing his own affairs even though the particular trustee may not be a man of business and may be wholly unsuited to his role as trustee.

The question arises whether a solicitor or accountant in a general High Street practice will be judged by a standard different from that of a solicitor or accountant trustee who is a member of a large city firm with a specialised trust department. In the author's view, the court would probably apply a different standard. The general practitioner would be judged by the minimum standard expected of a member of his profession by reference to section 1(1)(b), while the professional in a specialised department of a city firm would be expected to have a higher degree of experience and knowledge under subsection 1(1)(a).

The courts, in the context of professional negligence litigation, have for years been required to assess whether a professional has fallen below the standard of competence expected in his profession. A professional carrying on practice is expected to exercise a reasonable degree of skill and care. The standard of care will vary depending on the nature of the professional and his degree of expertise. In the case of *Duchess of Argyll v Beusilinck [1972] 2 Lloyd's Reports 172*, Megarry V-C considered the position of a specialist solicitor:

> 'No doubt the inexperienced solicitor is liable if he fails to attain the standard of a reasonably competent solicitor. But if the client employs a solicitor of high standing and great experience, will an action for negligence fail if it appears that the solicitor did not exercise the care and skill to be expected of him even though he did not fall below the standard of a reasonably competent solicitor? If the client engages an expert and doubtless expects to pay commensurate fees, is he not entitled to expect something more than the standard of the reasonably competent solicitor?'

The wording of section 1 of the Trustee Act 2000 gives the court plenty of scope to apply a case-by-case approach based on the facts of a particular case. It will be interesting to see how the court interprets and applies section 1. At the time of writing, no reported cases on section 1 have filtered through.

Fiduciary nature of power

4.11   A trustee's power of investment is a fiduciary power as opposed to a mere power. This means that the trustee is under a duty to the beneficiaries to consider its exercise, though he is not bound to exercise it. The power must be exercised with a single eye to the benefit of the beneficiaries – *Vestey's* (*Lord*) *Executors v IRC [1949] 1 All ER 1108 at 1115*. There, trustees were bound to invest in accordance with a direction from authorised persons under the terms of a trust deed. The Inland Revenue tried to argue that the authorised persons were interested in the settled property and therefore assessable to tax on the wording of the relevant statutory provision. The court held that as the power to direct investment was fiduciary in nature it could not be used to benefit the donees of the power and so they did not have an interest for the purpose of the relevant tax provision.

Ulterior purpose

4.12   Trustees must exercise their powers for the proper purpose. As stated in *Balls v Strutt (1841) 1 Hare 146 at 149* by Wigram V-C:

'A trustee shall not be permitted to use the powers which the law may confer upon him at law, except for the legitimate purpose of his trust . . .'.

The more recent cases of *Hayim v Citibank NA [1987] AC 730 at 746* and *Edge v Pensions Ombudsman [1998] Ch 512 at 535* restate this well-established rule. In the case of an investment power, the proper purpose must be to benefit the beneficiaries by generating a return of an income or capital nature. Therefore trustees should not make investment for an ulterior purpose. For example, it would be wrong for a trustee to invest in a company that a member of the trustee's family owned or controlled as a favour to that person.

In the same way, trustees should not make loans in order to accommodate third parties or even beneficiaries if this cannot be justified in investment terms. An old example of such a case is *Langston v Ollivant (1807) Copp G 33* where the executor and trustees were directed to hold a fund for the testator's daughter for life and thereafter for her children. They were directed to place the fund out on such real or personal security as should be thought to be good and sufficient. On the marriage of the testator's daughter to a Mr John Langston, they made a loan to him for the purpose of his trade. At the time he was prosperous enough. Years later his business failed and the loan was lost. The remainderman, a child of the life tenant, sued the trustees for breach of trust. The court held that the power of investment of the trustees did not permit them to make an accommodation which was what had happened in this case.

Question of morality

4.13   Trustees must not only disregard their own financial or family interest, they must also put aside their social and political opinions and motivations when making investments. They should not, therefore, let their own strong views on such matters as, for example, armaments or tobacco or animal testing, to influence them against making investments that are, in financial terms, suitable and beneficial to the trust fund – *Cowan v Scargill [1985] Ch 270*. There, Megarry V-C said that trustees must put the interests of their beneficiaries first and that the best interest of beneficiaries usually meant their best financial interests. He went on to say:

'In considering what investments to make trustees must put on one side their own personal interests and views. Trustees may have strongly held social or political views. They may be firmly opposed to any investment in South Africa or other countries, or they may object to any form of investment in companies concerned with alcohol, tobacco, armaments or many other things. In the conduct of their own affairs, of course, they are free to abstain from making any such investments. Yet under a trust if investment of this type would be more beneficial to the beneficiaries than other investments, the trustees must not refrain from making the investments by reason of the views that they hold'.

He then added the caveat that 'benefit' was a word of wide meaning and that benefit might not in every circumstance mean financial benefit, so that if all the beneficiaries of a trust were adults who held strict views on moral or social matters, it might not be for their benefit to know that their increased returns were being generated from tainted sources. However, such cases were likely to be rare and trustees would bear the burden proving that lesser returns were justified as a result of excluding some of the more profitable forms of investment.

In *Harries v Church Commissioners for England [1992] 1 WLR 1241* the plaintiffs sought declarations that the defendant Church Commissioners were obliged in managing the assets invested by them to have regard to the object of promoting the Christian faith through the established Church of England and might not act in a manner incompatible with that object. Sir Donald Nicholls V-C refused the declarations sought, holding that the discharge of their duty would normally require them to seek the maximum return that was consistent with commercial prudence. He said that there might be rare cases involving charities where certain investments would conflict with the objects of the charity, in which case trustees should not make such investment. There might also be rare cases where the trustees' holding of particular investments might hamper the work of the charity by making potential recipients of aid unwilling to be helped because of the source of the charity's money or by alienating some of those who supported the charity financially.

He went on to say that trustees might, if they wished, accommodate the views of those who considered that on moral grounds a particular investment would be in conflict with the objects of the charity, so long as the trustees were satisfied that the course would not involve a risk of significant financial detriment. But when they were not so satisfied, trustees should not make investment decisions on the basis of preferring one moral view over another. He emphasised that where questions of morality were concerned there was no identifiable yardstick which could be applied to a set of facts to yield one answer which could be seen to be 'right' and the other 'wrong'. Trustees were not to use property held by them for investment purposes as a means of making moral statements at the expense of the charity.

Even handedness

4.14   Trustees in exercising powers must hold an even hand among all the beneficiaries except in so far as the settlement authorises them to discriminate. In *Nestle v National Westminster Bank [2000] WTLR 795*, a case where a remainderman sued trustees for alleged breach of trust for failing to achieve a sufficiently good investment performance, at first instance Hoffmann J discussed the principle in the following terms:

> 'This brings me to the second principle on which there was general agreement, namely that the trustee must act fairly in making investment decisions which may have different consequences for different classes of beneficiaries. There are two reasons why I prefer this formulation to the traditional image of holding the scales equally between tenant for life and remainderman. The first is that the image of the scales suggests a weighing of known quantities whereas investment decisions are concerned with predictions of the future. Investments will carry current expectations of their future income yield and capital appreciation and these expectations will be reflected in their current market price, but there is always a greater or lesser risk that the outcome will deviate from those expectations. A judgment on the fairness of the choices made by the trustees must have regard to these imponderables. The second reason is that the image of the scales suggests a more mechanistic process than I believe the law requires. The trustees have in my judgment a wide discretion. They are for example entitled to take into account the income needs of the tenant for life or the fact that the tenant for life was a person known to the settlor and a primary object of the trust whereas the remainderman is a remoter relative or a stranger. Of course these cannot be allowed to become the overriding considerations but the concept of fairness between classes of beneficiaries does not require them to be excluded. It would be an inhuman law which required trustees to adhere to some mechanical rule for preserving the real value of the capital when the tenant for life was the testator's widow who had fallen upon hard times and the remainderman was young and well off'.

Trustees should not, therefore, in choosing investments, exercise that choice for the sole benefit of the tenant for life, by choosing investments that produce high income returns at the expense of security of capital. In the case of *Raby v Ridelhagh (1855) 7 De GM & G 104* trustees were persuaded by the life tenants of two shares in a trust fund to abandon their intention of investing in funds and instead to lay out the trust funds of the shares on mortgage so as to obtain the maximum possible income. The mortgages proved deficient and claims were made against the trustees. It was held that the trustees had acted in breach of trust because they made investments at the instance of the life tenants without considering the interest of the other beneficiaries. In *Stuart v Stuart (1841) 3 Beav 430* the terms of a will permitted the trustees to invest the will trust fund in the Public Funds of Great Britain or upon government funds or real securities in England or Wales. The life tenant widow applied to the court for an order permitting the trust fund to be invested on mortgages in Ireland which would produce greater income for her. The court refused the application on the grounds that it was not in the interests of the remaindermen for the fund to be so invested.

The rule in Howe v Earl of Dartmouth

4.15   Where residuary personal estate is settled by will for the benefit of persons interested in succession, all parts of it, which are of a wasting character or a future or reversionary nature or consist of unauthorised investments, ought to be converted into authorised investments of a permanent and income-bearing nature unless the will shows a contrary intention. This is known as the rule in *Howe v Earl of Dartmouth (1802) 7 Ves 137* and is a corollary of the rule that trustees must act even handedly between different classes of beneficiaries. If wasting property or property that produces a high income but with little capital security is retained, then this disadvantages the remaindermen and favours the life tenant. If reversionary property is not converted, then the remainderman will benefit at the expense of the life tenant.

The rule is confined to will trusts affecting residuary personal estate. It does not apply to *inter vivos* settlements nor does it apply to real estate because it is presumed that such property is meant to be enjoyed in specie. Nor does the rule apply to property that is specifically devised or bequeathed by will.

The rule in *Howe v Earl of Dartmouth* yields to a contrary intention shown in the will and thus does not apply if the will directs or impliedly provides that the life tenant is to enjoy the income from the property in specie, or the will confers on the trustees a discretion to postpone conversion not merely as an ancillary power for the more convenient realisation of the estate, but as an independent power for the benefit of the life tenant (*Re Berry [1962] Ch 97*). The burden of showing that the will contains a sufficient contrary intention lies on the person asserting that the rule in *Howe v Earl Dartmouth* should not be applied (*Macdonald v Irvine (1878) 8 Ch D 101 at 112; Re Wareham [1912] 2 Ch 312 at 315*).

The rule in *Howe v Earl of Dartmouth* also has a second part that requires apportionment between life tenant and remainderman. Where property ought to be converted and the proceeds invested either as being settled residuary personalty or being subject to an express trust for sale, the tenant for life is entitled pending conversion to the whole net income of income-producing property if a direction to that effect is expressed or can be implied from the terms of the will. In the absence of such a direction or implication the following rules apply:

*   the life tenant is entitled to the whole of the ordinary rent of real estate and of leasehold but not to mineral royalties (*Hope v D'Hedouville [1893] 2 Ch 361; Re Searle [1900] 2 Ch 829; Re Oliver [1908] 2 Ch 74*);

*   where property is personal estate (other than leasehold and authorised investments) the life tenant is only entitled to a fair equivalent of the income that he would have received if the property had been sold and

invested in authorised investments (*Brown v Gellatly (1867) 2 Ch App 751; Meyer v Simonsen (1852) 5 De G & Sm 723*);

- where property is of a reversionary nature the life tenant is entitled, when it falls in, to a proportionate part of the capital representing compound interest (with yearly rests) on the true actuarial value of the property at the date of the testator's death, calculated on the assumption that the actual date when the property fell into possession could have then been predicted with certainty (*Re Earl of Chesterfield's Trusts (1883) 24 Ch D 643; Re Goodenough [1895] 2 Ch 537; Re Hobson (1885) 53 LT 627*).

The second part of the rule in *Howe v Earl of Dartmouth* is not, like the first part, confined to settled residuary personalty. It is equally applicable to all settled property which is subject to a direction for sale exercisable forthwith. It does not apply, however, where a sale is directed at a future date. A mere power to postpone conversion is not, however, enough to constitute a direction for sale at a future date (*Re Berry [1962] Ch 97*).

The rule in *Howe v Earl of Dartmouth* obviously is capable of producing considerable inconvenience and so it, along with various other rules such as the rule in *Allhusen v Whittell* (which involves a life tenant being required to bear part of the expenses of administration of an estate), is generally excluded in all professionally drawn modern wills. A typical clause would be one that provided that:

'The income of the Trust Fund shall, however the property is invested, be treated and applied as income'.

The Standard Provisions of the Society of Trust and Estate Practitioners tackle the problem in a different way by including among the powers of the trustees a power to acquire wasting and non income-producing assets. As these investments are authorised investments, the rule in *Howe v Earl Dartmouth* has no application and it is unnecessary to exclude them (*Re Nicholson [1909] 2 Ch 111; Re Van Straubenzee, Boustead v Cooper [1901] 2 Ch 779*).

Stocks sold cum dividends

4.16   When trustees acquire stocks or shares on which dividends have been earned and declared but not paid at the date of purchase, such dividends must be carried to capital and not paid as income (*Re Sir Robert Peel's Settled Estates [1910] 1 Ch 389*). In the absence of special circumstances where stocks or shares are sold between two dividend days, no apportionment of income will be made (*Bulkeley v Stephens [1896] 2 Ch 241; Scholefield v Redfern (1862) 2 Drew & Sm 173; Re Henderson [1940] 1 All ER 623*).

In *Re MacLaren's Settlement Trusts [1951] 2 All ER 414* Harman J stated:

'The court can then in special circumstances apportion between capital and income on sale or purchases of stock cum dividend or ex dividend although it is not the practice to do so in the ordinary way because the various persons interested under settlements ought to take the rough with the smooth, and in order to ease the burden falling on trustees. The jurisdiction, however, exercised in special circumstances seems to be only the exercise of a right to make a more exact distinction of income from capital. As a matter of convenience the practice is in the ordinary case that no apportionments are made, with the result that capital sometimes gets what, on a more exact scrutiny, would prove to be income or vice versa. Where this produces a glaring injustice the court will cause a more exact calculation to be made, but it does not treat as income that which is capital or as capital that which is income'.

Third party directions and consents

4.17   Trust powers are not necessarily exercisable solely by trustees. Wills and settlements have for many years conferred powers on the settlor or beneficiaries or, indeed, on third parties. A power to direct investments is commonly conferred on parties other than the trustees. A power to direct investments is normally a fiduciary one.

In the case of *Vestey's (Lord) Executors v IRC [1949] 1 All ER 1108 at 1115*, Lord Simonds said that:

'Nothing short of the most direct and express words would, I think, justify a construction which would enable those who exercised the power of direction to disregard the interests of the beneficiaries'.

Vestey is, however, inconsistent with the earlier first instance case of *Re Hart's Will Trusts [1943] 2 All ER 557*. There the trustees were to invest the trust fund in such investments as the testatrix's son should direct, whether the same should be investments authorised by law for the investment of trust funds or not, and were to pay the income of the trust fund to the said son for his life. The trustees took out a summons to determine the extent of this power and whether they were permitted to purchase shares for the trust fund from the son at his direction and whether the son could direct them to sell investments in order to have money with which to purchase shares from the son. The court answered both questions affirmatively. Provided that the son acted in good faith, the trustees needed only to satisfy themselves that a reasonable price was being paid for the shares. It is questionable whether the same result would be reached today in the light of the *Vestey* decision given the lack of any clear wording permitting a self-dealing by the son of the nature contemplated in the *Hart* case.

Trustees, where they are directed to sell or purchase a particular asset at the request of a life tenant, are obliged to sell or purchase and have no discretion in the matter – *Re Hurst (1890) 63 LT 665* – provided that there is no objection on the score of the price.

Where a beneficiary was given a power to direct the trustees to purchase leaseholds generally, they were not obliged to invest in property in a low, bad and deteriorating situation (*Beauclerk v Ashburnham (1845) 8 Beav 322 at 328*).

If a beneficiary is required to consent to the sale of a trust asset, the beneficiary is not in a fiduciary position in giving or withholding consent and so is as free as anyone else to purchase the asset from the trustees (*Dicconson v Talbot (1870) 6 Ch App 32*). In the same way, trustees with a power with the consent of the tenant for life to lend trust funds on personal security were held to be free, if satisfied that there was a reasonable prospect of repayment, to lend them to the tenant for life on his personal security (*Re Laing's Settlement [1899] 1 Ch 593*).

Where trustees have a power of varying investments with the consent of the tenant for life, that power is given to the tenant for life for his own protection so that the trustees have an obligation to protect the interests of the persons interested in remainder (*Re Harrison v Thexton (1858) 4 Jur (NS) 550; Re Hotchkin's Settled Estates (1887) 35 Ch D 41*).

If the tenant for life's consent to a change in investment is required and he refuses to give that consent, then if the trust fund is being jeopardised, the trustees can apply to the court for power to sell the particular asset under section 57 of the Trustee Act 1925.

Giving consent a question of law and construction

4.18   The timing and manner of giving consent is a question of law and construction. If consent is required to be given in advance, it cannot be given retrospectively – *Bateman v Davis (1818) 3 Madd 98* where trustees had power to lend to the husband with the consent of the wife and lent at their own discretion without seeking prior consent. It was held that the consent could not be obtained after the event. On the other hand, in *Child v Child (1855) 20 Beav 50*, it was held that the consent of a wife to the exercise by trustees of a power to lend trust funds to her husband could not be given prospectively and the wife could not validly consent to trustees lending her husband trust funds at such times and in such proportions as he should require.

In the case of *Greenham v Gibbeson (1834) 10 Bing 363 at 374*, a consent was necessary for the substitution of one estate with another. It was held that the consent had to precede or be contemporaneous with the execution of the power of substitution because the question had to be determined by reference to the relative values of the two estates at the time of substitution.

A beneficiary is not taken to have consented to an investment merely by virtue of having joined in a deed of appointment of new trustees that recited or noted the investment (*Wiles v Gresham (1854) 2 Drew 258 at 267*). In order to show a valid consent it is necessary to show that the beneficiary had knowledge of the nature of the proposed investment (*Re Massingberd's Settlement* (*1890*) *63 LT 296; Re Pauling's Settlement [1964] Ch 303*).

If an investment is made without a required consent then an adult beneficiary of full capacity may be held to have acquiesced in it if he adopts it or obtains full knowledge of it and makes no objection to it (*Stevens v Robertson* (*1868*) *37 LJ Ch 499*).

A special principle derived from employment law applies in the field of trusts of pension schemes. Where employers have powers under scheme trust deeds and rules, they are subject to the implied limitation that their powers cannot be exercised in a manner that will knowingly injure the relationship of trust and confidence that ought to exist between employer and employee (*Imperial Group Pension Trust Ltd v Imperial Tobacco Ltd [1991] 1 WLR 589; British Coal Corporation v British Coal Staff Superannuation Scheme Trustees Ltd [1994] ICR 537*).

Chapter 5

Investment in Land

The old law and reform

5.1   In Part VIII of the Law Commission's Consultation Paper entitled 'Trustees' Powers and Duties', the old law that applied prior to the introduction of the Trustee Act 2000 was summarised in the following terms:

'In the absence of express authority in the trust instrument, trustees of personal property do not have power either to invest in the purchase of land or to acquire land as a residence or otherwise for the use of any beneficiary. By contrast where land is held in trust, whether under a trust of land or a settlement under the Settled Land Act 1925 the trustees have power to purchase more land not only by way of investment but for any other reason'.

The powers of trustees of a Settled Land Act settlement arose under section 73 of the Settled Land Act 1925. The powers of trustees of a trust of land arose under sections 6(3) and 17(1) of the Trusts of Land and Appointment of Trustees Act 1996, as originally enacted. Both provisions have been amended by the Trustee Act 2000.

The Law Commission considered that there was no rational justification for the position under the old law and proposed that trustees should have a default power to purchase land in England and Wales by way of investment, for occupation by a beneficiary or for any other reason. The Law Commission felt that the territorial limitation that applied to the old law should continue to apply and that if settlors wished to confer power on trustees to acquire land outside England and Wales, they should do so by way of express provision. This meant that the general power of investment that was proposed to be introduced by the Trustee Act 2000 would need to be modified in relation to land because the general power enables a trustee to make any kind of investment that he could make if he were absolutely entitled to the trust assets. The continued restriction on the acquisition of foreign land was justified because many foreign jurisdictions do not recognise the concept of the trust and the Law Commission felt that this might lead to difficulties whereby successful claims by creditors or spouses of trustees might be brought against the trust assets notwithstanding that such trustees were never intended themselves to have any beneficial claim to the land in question.

Trustee Act 2000

The general power of investment

5.2   Section 3 of the Trustee Act 2000, which concerns the general power of investment, provides by subsection (3) thereof that the general power does not permit a trustee to make investments in land other than in loans secured on land. Reference is, however, made to section 8.

Section 8 provides as follows:

'(1) A trustee may acquire freehold or leasehold land in the United Kingdom—

(a)   as an investment,

(b)   for occupation by a beneficiary, or

(c)   for any other reason.

(2) "Freehold or leasehold land" means—

(a)   in relation to England and Wales, a legal estate in land,

(b)   in relation to Scotland—

   (i)   the estate or interest of the proprietor of the dominium utile or, in the case of land not held on feudal tenure, the estate or interest of the owner, or

   (ii)   a tenancy, and

(c)   in relation to Northern Ireland, a legal estate in land, including land held under a fee farm grant.

(3) For the purpose of exercising his functions as a trustee, a trustee who acquires land under this section has all the powers of an absolute owner in relation to the land.'

Section 9 provides that the powers conferred by Part III of the Act (ie section 8) are in addition to powers conferred on trustees other than by Part III but subject to any restriction or exclusion imposed by the trust instrument or by any enactment or any provision of subordinate legislation.

Section 10 provides that Part III of the Act applies to trusts whether created before or after the commencement of the Act on 1 February 2001. The section applies to personal representatives. Section 8 does not apply to strict settlements that remain governed by the Settled Land Act 1925 nor does it apply to trusts governed by the Universities and College Estates Act 1925. Section 8 does not apply to pension schemes (see section 36 of the Trustee Act 2000) nor does it apply to authorised unit trusts (section 37) nor to common investment schemes under the Charities Act 1993 (section 38).

By virtue of section 6(3) of the Trusts of Land and Appointment of Trustees Act 1996, trustees of land have power to acquire land under the power conferred by section 8 of the Trustee Act 2000. The section, as originally enacted, was amended by the Trustee Act 2000 to bring it into line with the 2000 Act.

Definition of land

5.3   The Trustee Act 2000 does not define the term 'land'. The Law of Property Act 1925 definition is not used. The position contrasts with the Trusts of Land and Appointment of Trustees Act 1996 which uses the Law of Property Act definition (see section 22(3) of the 1996 Act). Therefore, under the Trustee Act 2000, the definition in the Interpretation Act 1978 applies. Section 5 and Schedule 1 to that Act define land as including 'buildings and other structures, land covered with water and any estate, interest, easement, servitude or right in or over land'.

The exclusion of investments in land from the general power of investment under section 3 therefore prevents investments in land as defined above. The exclusion prevents investments in interests in land, eg beneficial shares in land under a trust of land or other equitable interests such as a reversionary interest. Also excluded are rights in land such as easements or rent charges. Foreign land would be covered by the exclusion, although if the law of a foreign jurisdiction retains the doctrine of conversion whereby land is regarded as converted to the proceeds of land, an interest in foreign land might not be covered if the *lex situs* regarded the interest as an interest in personalty.

The exclusion of investments in land from the general power of investment under section 3 would not prevent trustees from investing in the shares or stock of a company that held land. Security interests in land are permitted under section 3(3) if they constitute loans secured on land. Section 3(4) provides that a person invests in a loan secured on land if he has rights under any contract under which one person provides another with credit, and the obligation of the borrower to repay is secured on land. Credit is defined as any cash loan or other financial accommodation. Cash is defined as including money in any form.

The power under section 8 is a power to acquire land and is not restricted to purchases and so exchanges would be included as well. Only land in the United Kingdom is covered by the power. Further, trustees can only acquire legal estates, ie freehold land or leaseholds. Equitable interests in land or undivided equitable shares are not permitted. Presumably, however, so long as trustees take the legal estate, it is possible for them to hold that estate on trust for their beneficiaries as to a proportion of the equitable interest and for third parties as to the remaining proportion of the equitable interest.

Further, section 8 will presumably not be interpreted in such a way as to prevent trustees from acquiring land under the usual two-stage contract procedure, whereby they would acquire an equitable interest on execution of the contract but legal title would not be acquired until completion when a transfer was executed and registered. In the same way, it is unlikely that section 8 was intended to prevent trustees from entering into options to purchase or sell land.

Duty of care

5.4   Section 2 and Schedule 1 to the Trustee Act 2000 apply the statutory duty of care to a trustee when exercising the statutory power under section 8 to acquire land or when exercising any other power to acquire land, however conferred. The duty of care also applies when trustees exercise any power in relation to land acquired under the statutory power or an express power (Sch 1, para 2(c)). Under section 8(3) a trustee who acquires land under section 8 has all the powers of an absolute owner and so any acts of management of the land would seem to be subject to the new statutory duty of care.

If land is acquired as an investment, in other words, to generate a return of an income or capital nature, then the trustees are obliged to have regard to the standard investment criteria under section 4 and to assess whether land is a suitable addition to the trust's portfolio of investments and whether the particular land in question is a suitable investment. They are also obliged under section 5 to take and consider appropriate advice. The general safeguards therefore apply to an investment in land as they do to other types of investments. The 2000 Act does not specify, for example, the minimum unexpired length of term required of any leasehold acquired, but rather relies on the general safeguards to exclude unsuitable properties. The acquisition of a short leasehold term will, in most cases, be an unsuitable investment. Short leaseholds will also be inconsistent with the trustees' duty to hold an even hand between life tenant and remaindermen.

Occupation by a beneficiary

5.5   Under section 8(1)(b) land can be acquired for the purpose of occupation by a beneficiary. Under the general law, trustees were not permitted to acquire land for the purposes of occupation by a beneficiary by exercise of a power of investment. This is because land acquired for such a use is not an investment – see *Re Power, Public Trustee v Hastings [1947] Ch 572*. Section 8 therefore provides an important default power to trustees. Trustees of trusts of land had a similar power under section 6(4) of the Trusts of Land and Appointment of Trustees Act 1996 in its original form. Section 8 is intended to be an administrative power and not a dispositive power and so it should not be taken as conferring interests or rights on beneficiaries more extensive than they enjoy under the beneficial provisions of the settlement in question.

The most appropriate situation in which the power could be exercised would be that of an interest in possession trust, where a beneficiary entitled to the income from the fund is given a right to occupy a property purchased by the trustees. However, a beneficiary under a discretionary trust might also be allowed to occupy property in exercise of the trustees' discretion. It would not be appropriate for trustees to purchase a property for occupation by a beneficiary with a reversionary interest.

If property is acquired for the occupation of a beneficiary then there is no requirement to have regard to the standard investment criteria, nor is there a need to take investment advice for the purpose of section 5 of the Trustee Act 2000. However, the statutory duty of care applies and so trustees would be obliged to ensure that the property was acquired at a sensible price and was structurally sound and otherwise suitable for the purpose of occupation by the beneficiary in question. In order to discharge their duty, trustees would need to obtain a proper valuation of the land before committing themselves to acquiring it for a given price. Further, they ought, in most cases, to obtain a suitable survey to determine the condition of the land and whether any liabilities affect it. The trustees would also have to ensure that the exercise by them of the power to acquire property for occupation by a beneficiary was consistent with their duty to treat all beneficiaries in an even handed manner.

The purchase of chattels

5.6   The power in section 8 does not enable trustees to purchase chattels for use by a beneficiary in the property. It would not, therefore, be possible for trustees to use the power under section 8 to purchase furniture unless the purchase was merely incidental to the purchase of the property itself. However, some fitting out of the property might be permissible on the ground that it was incidental to the exercise of the main power. Trustees, where possible, could use a power of advancement in order to purchase furniture in order to avoid difficulties of this sort. The purchase of chattels would not ordinarily qualify as an investment unless such chattels were, for example, antiques that could be expected to appreciate in value.

Personal representatives

5.7   Section 35 of the Trustee Act 2000 applies section 8 to personal representatives. However, section 35(2)(c) provides that the reference to a beneficiary in section 8(1)(b) is to be read as a reference to a person who, under the will of the deceased or under the law relating to intestacy, is beneficially interested in the estate. This contrasts with the more general provision under section 35(2)(b) whereby references to a beneficiary or to beneficiaries are, in general, to be read as references to a person or the persons interested in the due administration of the estate.

The drafting of this section leaves a lot to be desired. It seems to be trying to make clear that personal representatives should only have a power to acquire land for occupation by beneficiaries who have an interest under a will or intestacy. However, case law has established that a beneficiary of an estate in the course of administration does not technically have a beneficial interest in the estate. The whole legal and beneficial interest in the assets of the estate remains vested in the personal representatives (*Marshall v Kerr [1995] 1 AC 148; Commissioner of Stamp Duties (Queensland) v Livingston [1964] 3 All ER 692*). All that an estate beneficiary has is a *chose in action*, that being the right to compel due administration of the estate.

The distinction drawn between subsections (2)(b) and (2)(c) is therefore somewhat difficult to apply. It is true that not only beneficiaries have an interest in due administration; creditors of an estate are also entitled to insist on due administration and so the general provision in section 35(2)(b) would include them, but under section 35(2)(c) they would be excluded.

However, there are surely no circumstances in which it would be proper for a personal representative to acquire property for occupation by a creditor and so it is difficult to see that the distinction between creditors and beneficiaries is what the draftsman was driving at. If the true distinction that was intended was between a person with significant interests under a will or intestacy and those with a lesser interest, then the wording does not achieve this. A legatee with a small pecuniary legacy is 'interested in the estate' and yet it is difficult to see in what circumstances it would be appropriate to acquire land for occupation by such a beneficiary. Nor does the wording in section 35(2)(c) limit the power to residuary beneficiaries. In practice, it will only be an appropriate exercise of the personal representatives' powers under section 8(1)(b) as a matter of general trust law if they use the power in favour of beneficiaries with a significant interest under the will or intestacy. It may, however, be useful for personal representatives to have such a power in that they may need to acquire a residence for, say, a widow or a minor beneficiary at a time before an estate administration is completed and a will trust is constituted. The power will enable personal representatives to take urgent action without needing to concern themselves with the question of whether they have become trustees in a technical sense.

Power to acquire land for other purposes

5.8   Under section 8(1)(c) of the Trustee Act 2000, trustees may acquire land for any other reason apart from that of investment or occupation by a beneficiary. The acquisition of land would, however, need to be incidental to the exercise by the trustees of their other powers. Section 8(1)(c) would, for example, enable trustees who were empowered to run a business to acquire premises to be used for the purpose of the business. Trustees, however, need an express power permitting them to carry on a business in the first place.

A further example of a situation in which section 8(1)(c) might be used would be that of a non-charitable unincorporated association where land might be acquired and held by trustees for the purposes of the association. Also conceivable is where a large private trust might need to acquire office premises from which to conduct the trust's administration. There might also be 'Quistclose-type' commercial purpose trusts that require land to be acquired as part of the purpose involved – for further explanation of what a Quistclose trust involves, see *Barclays Bank v Quistclose Investments Ltd [1970] AC 567; Twinsectra v Yardley [2002] 2 AC 164*.

Section 8(3) provides that a trustee who acquires land under the power in section 8 has all the powers of an absolute owner for the purposes of exercising his functions as a trustee. This is in similar terms to section 6(1) of the Trusts of Land and Appointment of Trustees Act 1996 which gives trustees of land the powers of an absolute owner. Once land is acquired by trustees in exercise of their section 8 power, the trust in question will become a trust of land within the definition in section 1 of the 1996 Act which defines a trust of land as 'any trust of property which consists of or includes land'.

Section 8(3) of the 2000 Act therefore seems designed to run hand in hand with section 6(1) of the 1996 Act. Arguably, it was unnecessary to include section 8(3) since the acquisition of land by trustees brings the 1996 Act into play anyway. However, the inclusion of section 8(3) should, if nothing else, put an end to the possibility of any arid debate as to whether trustees have power to mortgage land in order to acquire it.

In the case of *Abbey National v Cann [1991] 1 AC 56*, the House of Lords analysed a purchase with the aid of a mortgage as being one indivisible transaction and rejected the previous view stated in earlier cases that there were two distinct transactions, ie purchase of the legal estate and the grant of a mortgage over it separated by a *scintilla temporis*. The wording of section 8(3) would allow trustees to acquire land with the aid of a mortgage over the land being acquired.

By having the powers of an absolute owner, trustees have very wide powers to lease, mortgage and sell land. Section 8(3) will also allow trustees to hold land jointly with other persons. However, because trustees are empowered to acquire only legal estates in land, it will be necessary for trustees to acquire the legal title. It will not be possible for them to acquire just a beneficial share.

Express powers

5.9   Section 9 of the Trustee Act 2000 provides that the default power in section 8 is additional to powers otherwise conferred on trustees but is subject to any restriction or exclusion imposed by the trust instrument. In considering any express power relating to the acquisition of land it will be necessary to analyse whether it is wider or narrower than the statutory power. An express power might allow trustees to acquire land in a foreign jurisdiction or to acquire an interest less than a legal estate, such as a beneficial share in a property. Alternatively, an express power might limit the purposes for which land can be acquired.

A typical modern investment power in beneficial owner form will authorise the acquisition of land as an investment (*Re Peczenik's Settlement Trusts [1964] 1 WLR 720*). Older forms of investment clauses commonly authorised investment by way of loans secured on land. This sort of power did not actually authorise the acquisition of land – see *Re Mordan, Legg v Mordan [1905] 1 Ch 515*. A power to invest 'on real security' does not authorise the purchase of land.

In *Re Suenson-Taylor's Settlement [1974] 1 WLR 1280* trustees had a wide power of investment in beneficial owner terms. It read:

> 'The trustees shall have the same unrestricted power of investment of moneys requiring investment under the trusts hereof as they would have if they were a sole absolute and beneficial owner of the trust fund . . .'.

The trustees held land as part of the trust investments. They wished to mortgage that land in order to acquire further land for investment purposes. They applied to the court for a declaration that they had the power to do so under the terms of the settlement or, alternatively, by virtue of section 16 of the Trustee Act 1925.

Foster J held that the money requiring investment for the purposes of the investment power fell into three categories on the proper construction of the settlement:

(*a*)   the original £2,000 settled when the settlement was created;

(*b*)   the proceeds of sale of investment; and

(*c*)   any new cash put into the settlement after it has been executed.

He went on to hold that the terms of the settlement did not authorise the proposed borrowing since there was no capital cash falling within the three categories identified by him and which was required to be invested within the terms of the investment power. He also held that section 16 of the Trustee Act 1925 did not authorise the proposed borrowing.

An express power to invest money in the purchase of land will not permit land to be acquired for a wider purpose such as occupation by a beneficiary as in *Re Power, Public Trustee v Hastings [1947] Ch 572*. There the Public Trustee had, under the testator's will, a wide power of investment in beneficial owner terms. The widow tenant for life asked the trustee to purchase a dwelling house for occupation by her and the testator's children. The trustee asked the court for a direction whether he had power to purchase a property for this purpose. The court held that the trustee did not have such a power because it would not constitute an investment. In the same way, an express power to purchase land for occupation by a beneficiary will not permit land to be acquired as an investment.

Duty of care

5.10   As noted above, the new statutory duty of care applies to trustees exercising a power to acquire land, whether the power is statutory or otherwise conferred. In most, if not all cases, it will be necessary for the trustees to obtain a proper professional valuation of the land in question and it may well be appropriate in many cases to obtain a structural survey. Trustees will also need to ensure that they employ a properly qualified person to handle the conveyancing aspects of the acquisition in order to ensure that good title is obtained and that any defects in title are so far as possible revealed. They should take care not to commit themselves to any unusual or unduly onerous contractual provisions. Under section 8 of the Trustee Act 2000, trustees only have power to acquire freehold or leasehold land and this is defined as a legal estate in land. It is therefore important that legal title to the land being acquired is obtained.

Trusts of Land and Appointment of Trustees Act 1996

5.11   Once trustees acquire land, the trust will become a trust of land within the definition in section 1(1) of the Trusts of Land and Appointment of Trustees Act 1996 (TLATA 1996). A trust of land is a trust of property that consists of or includes land. It is necessary for trustees to have a grasp of the material provisions in the Act that might affect them in their management of land acquired as an investment or for occupation by a beneficiary.

Background

5.12   The 1996 Act introduced a unitary system of trusts of land and put an end to the threefold division between Settled Land Act settlements, trusts for sale and bare trusts that formerly existed. The 1996 Act applies to express, implied, resulting and constructive trusts, trusts for sale and bare trusts – see section 1(2)(a) of the 1996 Act. The Act applies to trusts whether created before or after 1 January 1997, which is the date the Act came into force. The Act does not, however, apply to Settled Land Act settlements that existed prior to 1 January 1997, nor does it apply to land which is subject to the Universities and College Estates Act 1925. It is, however, impossible to create new settlements under the Settled Land Act 1925 after 1 January 1997. Land is defined by reference to the definition in the Law of Property Act 1925 (see TLATA 1996, s 23(2)) and, therefore, means land of any tenure and mines and minerals, whether or not held apart from the surface, buildings or parts of buildings (whether the division is horizontal or vertical or made in any other way) and other corporeal hereditaments; also a manor, an advowson, and a rent and other incorporeal hereditaments and an easement, right, privilege or benefit in, over or derived from land.

Express trusts for sale of land take effect as trusts of land after 1997. Trustees of such a trust have an implied power to postpone sale and this overrides any provision in the disposition creating the trust (TLATA 1996, s 4(1)). Trustees of a trust for sale remain subject to an obligation to sell but any trustee or person with an interest under the trust can apply to the court under sections 14 and 15 to prevent a sale. The settlor's wishes will be one of the factors that a court takes into account when deciding whether to enforce a sale or not.

The 1996 Act abolished the doctrine of conversion by which land held on trust for sale was regarded as an interest in personalty. The doctrine continues to apply to any trust created by the will of a person who died before 1997 or to the deceased personal representatives in the administration of his estate (whether he died testate or intestate).

Trustees of land have, for the purpose of exercising their functions as trustees, all the powers of an absolute owner (see TLATA 1996, s 6(1)). This absolute owner power extends only to land held under the trust and not to personal property held as part of the trust fund. The power is fiduciary and is administrative in nature and not dispositive. The statutory duty of care under the Trustee Act 2000 applies to trustees exercising their power under section 6 of TLATA 1996.

Under subsection (2) of section 6, where each of the beneficiaries of a trust of land is of full age and capacity and absolutely entitled, the trustees have the power to convey the land to the beneficiaries even though they have not been required to do so. Where land is conveyed under subsection (2), the beneficiaries must do whatever is necessary to secure that the land vests in them and, if they fail to do this, the court may make an order requiring them to do so. 'Beneficiary' is defined in section 22 as any person who under the trust has an interest in property subject to the trust (including a person who has an interest as a trustee or personal representative). A company would fall within such a definition as a company is a person according to the Interpretation Act 1978, s 5, Sch 1. Clearly, section 6(2) will cover the case where a number of beneficiaries are entitled as tenants in common where each of those persons is of full age and capacity and absolutely entitled. It would also seem to cover the case where only one beneficiary is entitled. However, in such a case trustees probably would not need statutory authority to convey the land to the beneficiary (see Megarry & Wade, *The Law of Real Property* (6th edn) Sweet & Maxwell (at p 448). Section 6(2) would not, as a matter of construction, seem to apply to the case where a life tenant and a remainderman are together absolutely entitled. The intention of Parliament was certainly that the section should apply to concurrent interests (see 571 HL Official Report (5th Series) Col 957). The section is designed to enable trustees to put an end to their trust and to free themselves from their obligations. It will enable property to be forced on beneficiaries against their will.

Section 7 of TLATA 1996 gives trustees the power to partition land where beneficiaries of full age are absolutely entitled in undivided shares to land. There is an ancillary power to provide by way of mortgage or otherwise for the payment of equality money. Before exercising their powers under section 7, the trustees must obtain the consent of each of the beneficiaries.

Under section 8(1) of TLATA 1996, it is provided that sections 6 and 7 do not apply to trusts of land created by a disposition in so far as the disposition makes provision to that effect. Section 8(2) provides that the powers in sections 6 and 7 may be made subject to consent by a term in the disposition creating the trust.

Section 9 of TLATA 1996 enables trustees of trusts of land to delegate their functions to a beneficiary of full age and beneficially entitled to an interest in possession in land subject to the trust.

Consultation

5.13   Section 11 of TLATA 1996 provides that trustees of land shall in the exercise of their functions relating to land subject to the trust:

(a)   so far as practicable, consult the beneficiaries of full age and beneficially entitled to an interest in possession in the land, and

(b)   so far as consistent with the general interest of the trust, give effect to the wishes of those beneficiaries, or (in case of dispute) of the majority (according to the value of their combined interests).

This obligation applies to all trusts of land created after 1996 except where the disposition provides to the contrary or where the trust arises under a will made before 1997, even if the testator dies after 1996. The duty to consult does not apply to trusts created prior to 1 January 1997 unless provision that it should apply is made by deed executed by the settlor who is of full age and capacity, or, where more than one person created the trust, by such of them as are alive and of full capacity. The trustees are not merely required to take into account the wishes of the beneficiaries; they are obliged to give effect to them so far as consistent with the general interest of the trust. They would therefore need to establish a cogent reason for going against the wishes of the beneficiaries or, where appropriate, a majority of them.

There is now a difference between trusts created before 1997, which now take effect as trusts of land, and trusts of land created after 1996. As regards the former, trustees are now under no obligation to consult the beneficiaries about the exercise of their powers even in relation to trusts where prior to 1997 such a duty existed. Section 26(3) of the Law of Property Act 1925 imposed a duty of consultation on trustees of trusts for sale created by or pursuant to the Law of Property Act 1925 or any other Act. The duty also applied to non-statutory trusts for sale if the disposition creating the trust showed an intention that the duty should apply. Section 26(3) was repealed by the Trusts of Land and Appointment of Trustees Act 1996 without any saving. This appears to have been an oversight. Beneficiaries under trusts of land do, however, now have the right to apply to the court under section 14 and on such an application the courts have to take into account the wishes of the beneficiaries of full age who are entitled to an interest in possession.

The section provides for the trustees to give effect to the wishes of the majority according to the value of their combined interests. This raises the question whether a person with a life interest in a percentage share of a property (for example, 25%) is entitled to have their wishes counted according to a simple 25% or whether their interest should be actuarially valued, in which case the interest of a female life tenant with an interest in a 25% share might outweigh the interest of a male life tenant of a similar age in another 25% share. It seems unlikely that the draftsman intended that the values of beneficiaries should be actuarially valued so as to give the interests of certain life tenants greater weight depending on their age and sex. Presumably, a more simple approach was intended whereby the percentage share itself is looked at for the purpose of establishing a majority.

The right to occupy

5.14   Prior to 1997, the position in relation to the rights of occupation of beneficiaries under trusts was as follows:

- a tenant for life under the Settled Land Act 1925 was entitled to occupy the land as an incident of the legal ownership that was vested in him;

- beneficiaries who enjoyed successive interests under a trust for sale could be allowed to occupy as a matter of the trustees' discretion;

- beneficiaries with concurrent interests under a trust for sale normally had the right to occupy the land pending sale unless there was an indicator to the contrary;

- a beneficiary under a bare trust was entitled to occupy because the trustees held the land as nominees to his order.

After 1 January 1997, section 12(1) of TLATA 1996 confers a statutory right of occupation on a beneficiary who is entitled to an interest in possession in land subject to a trust if at that time:

(a)   the purposes of the trust include making the land available for his occupation (or for the occupation of beneficiaries of a class of which he is a member or of beneficiaries in general), or

(b)   the land is held by the trustees so as to be so available.

Section 12(1) does not confer a right to occupy where land is either unavailable or unsuitable for occupation by the beneficiary. Section 12 is subject to section 13.

Section 13(1) provides that where two or more beneficiaries are (or, apart from this section, would be) entitled under section 12 to occupy land, the trustees of land may exclude or restrict the entitlement of any one or more (but not all) of them. Section 13(2) provides that trustees may not unreasonably exclude any beneficiary's entitlement to occupy land or restrict such an entitlement to an unreasonable extent.

Under section 13(3), trustees may impose reasonable conditions on any beneficiary in relation to his occupation of land by reason of his entitlement under section 12. In exercising their powers under section 13, the trustees must have regard to the following matters listed in subsection (4):

(a)   the intentions of the person or persons (if any) who created the trust,

(b)   the purposes for which the land is held, and

(c)   the circumstances and wishes of each of the beneficiaries who is (or apart from any previous exercise by the trustees of those powers would be) entitled to occupy the land under section 12.

The above list is not exhaustive. The conditions which might be imposed under subsection (3) include conditions as to payment of outgoings, or the assumption of any other obligations in relation to the land or to any present or proposed future activity on the land. For example, trustees can require a beneficiary to repair and decorate or to ensure that planning permission is complied with or that the land is not used so as to cause a nuisance to others.

Section 13(6) provides that where the entitlement of any beneficiary to occupy land has been excluded or restricted, the conditions which may be imposed on any other beneficiary include conditions requiring him to make payments by way of compensation to the beneficiary whose entitlements have been excluded or restricted or to forgo any payment or other benefit to which he would otherwise be entitled under the trust so as to benefit that beneficiary.

The powers under section 13 cannot be used to prevent any person who is in occupation of land (whether or not by reason of any entitlement under section 12) from continuing to occupy the land or in a manner likely to result in any such person ceasing to occupy the land unless he consents or the court has given approval. The court, in considering whether or not to give approval under subsection (7), is directed to consider the same matters as trustees have to consider under subsection (4), ie the intention of the person who created the trust, the purposes for which the land is held, the circumstances and wishes of the beneficiaries who are entitled to occupy. Although the beneficiary's occupation cannot be terminated directly or indirectly through the power to exclude, restrict or impose conditions, the trustees are entitled to terminate that occupation if the beneficiary ceases to have the right to occupy the land. This may be either because he ceases to be beneficially entitled to an interest in possession in the land or the conditions upon which that right depends are no longer satisfied, eg because the land has ceased to be suitable for occupation by the beneficiary.

Applications to court

5.15   Under section 14 of TLATA 1996, any person who is a trustee or has an interest in a property subject to a trust of land may make an application to the court for a court order. Under section 14 the court may make such order as it thinks fit relating to the exercise by the trustees of any of their functions (including an order relieving them of any obligation to obtain the consent of, or to consult, any person in connection with the exercise of any of their functions) or declaring the nature or extent of a person's interest in property subject to the trust. The court's power to declare interests under section 14 does not enable it to vary or create interests.

Section 15 lists the matters which the court must take into account. They include:

(a)   the intentions of the person or persons (if any) who created the trust,

(b)   the purposes for which the property subject to the trust is held,

(c)   the welfare of any minor who occupies or might reasonably be expected to occupy any land subject to the trust as his home, and

(d)   the interests of any secured creditor of any beneficiary.

In the case of an application relating to the exercise by trustees of their powers of restriction and exclusion etc under section 13, the court is also to have regard to the circumstances and wishes of each of the beneficiaries who is (or apart from any previous exercise by the trustees of those powers would be) entitled to occupy the land under section 12. In the case of any other application, other than one relating to the trustees' power under section 6(2) to convey land to beneficiaries, the matters to which the court is to have regard also include the circumstances and wishes of any beneficiaries of full age and entitled to an interest in possession in property subject to the trust or (in the case of dispute) of the majority (according to the value of their combined interests). Section 15 does not apply if section 335A of the Insolvency Act 1986 applies to it. That section concerns applications by a trustee in bankruptcy for realisation of a bankrupt's interest in a property held under a trust of land.

The intentions of the settlor who created the trust are just one of the factors that the court is directed to consider. They are not therefore paramount and each case will turn on its own facts.

Under the law that applied prior to the introduction of TLATA 1996, the courts, on applications made under section 30 of the Law of Property Act 1925, were used to considering the underlying purpose of the trust for sale on which land was held. They considered whether the object of the trust was indeed to sell the land or was in fact to retain it for a collateral purpose – for example, see *Jones v Challenger [1961] 1 QB 176; Harris v Harris (1995) 72 P & CR 408*. Many of the cases concerned couples where the property had been bought for the purpose of providing a home for the couple and their children. The court's powers under section 30 were more limited than under section 14 of TLATA 1996. Under section 30, the court could give effect to a trust for sale by ordering sale of the property. It could not impose terms on the parties directly. However, in many cases, judges gave an indication that a sale would be ordered unless the party in occupation offered to pay an occupation rent or make other compensation. After 1996 the court can act directly to impose such a result on the parties.

Chapter 6

Investment on Mortgage

Loans secured on land

6.1   Section 3 of the Trustee Act 2000, which provides the general power of investment, enables trustees to invest in loans secured on land. This is clear from the terms of subsection (3) which provides that the general power does not permit a trustee to make investments in land 'other than in loans secured on land'. Section 3(4) provides that a person invests in a loan secured on land if he has any rights under any contract under which one person provides another with credit and the obligation to repay is secured on land. 'Credit' is defined as any cash loan or other form of financial accommodation. Cash includes money in any form. 'Land', for the purposes of the Trustee Act 2000, bears the meaning given to it by the Interpretation Act 1978 rather than the definition in section 205 of the Law of Property Act 1925. It therefore includes 'buildings and other structures land covered with water and any estate, interest, easement, servitude or right in or over land'.

An investment on mortgage made by trustees in exercise of the section 3 power will be subject to the statutory duty of care. The duty to take appropriate advice in section 5 will apply as will the duty to have regard to the standard investment criteria in section 4. The duty to review investments under section 4 will also apply. In considering how the duty of care and the other statutory duties will be applied by the courts, it is useful to consider the old law that applied prior to 2000.

The law prior to 2000

6.2   Section 8(1) of the Trustee Act 1925 which has been repealed by the Trustee Act 2000 provided:

> 'A trustee lending money on the security of any property on which he can properly lend shall not be chargeable with breach of trust by reason only of the proportion borne by the amount of the loan to the value of the property at the time when the loan was made, if it appears to the Court—
>
> (a)   that in making the loan the trustee was acting upon a report as to the value of the property made by a person whom he reasonably believed

to be an able practical surveyor or valuer instructed and employed independently of any owner of the property, whether such surveyor or valuer carried on business in the locality where the property is situated or elsewhere; and

(b)   that the amount of the loan does not exceed two third parts of the value of the property as stated in the report; and

(c)   that the loan was made under the advice of the surveyor or valuer expressed in the report'.

While trustees could, under the 2000 Act, lend more than two-thirds of the value of the property and could, if they thought appropriate, dispense with advice, such a course of action would be at their own risk, whereas a trustee staying within the terms of the old section 8 would almost certainly be held to have discharged his duty of care. Section 8 of the Trustee Act 1925 re-enacted section 8 of the Trustee Act 1893 which was intended to provide guidance to trustees by laying down rules that constituted a standard by which reasonable conduct could be judged. Section 8 was itself a re-enactment of section 4 of the Trustee Act 1888. Prior to that Act, various cases had laid down guidance to trustees and the principles established by those cases were given statutory force by the passing of the 1888 Act. The two-thirds of the value rule was a rule first established by the courts and represented the courts' view of how a prudent trustee should approach a secured loan transaction. While trustees no doubt now have a greater degree of flexibility, the old section 8 was rooted in common sense and, in general, trustees after 2000 would be wise to stick to the two-thirds rule.

After 1 February 2001, the Trustee Act 2000 came into force. The Act frees trustees from their statutory straitjacket but they must still act with common prudence in order to discharge their duty of care.

Section 8 protection

6.3   To obtain the protection of section 8, the trustee must have obtained a valuation report as indicated by the section. This had to have been made by a person whom the trustee believed to have been a competent practical surveyor or valuer. The trustee must have exercised his own judgement in the choice of the surveyor or valuer – *Re Walker (1890) 59 LJ Ch 386*. It was not sufficient for the choice to be left to the trustee's solicitor – *Fry v Tapson (1884) 28 Ch D 268*. The surveyor need not have been possessed of special knowledge of the locality in which the property was situated, although of course, if a surveyor does possess such local knowledge, so much the better. The statute required that the valuer or surveyor should be independent from the owner of the property (*Re Duke of Somerset [1894] 1 Ch 231; Re Dive [1909] 1 Ch 328*). If the surveyor's fee is dependent on the transaction successfully completing then he cannot be said to be independent. There is some uncertainty as to whether the surveyor or valuer has to be objectively independent or whether a subjective belief on the part of the trustee that he is independent is enough – *In Re Solomon [1912] 1 Ch*

261 suggests that a subjective belief is enough. This, however, conflicts with the statement in *Re Duke of Somerset [1894] 1 Ch 231* where it was said that the valuer must be independent in fact. To provide protection, the report of the valuer must do more than just state the value. The loan will need to have been made under the advice of the surveyor or valuer and so the report must state what amount may safely be advanced on the security of the particular property. The two-thirds of value limit represents the maximum limit. A surveyor or valuer ought, however, to express a view on what sum can be lent.

Section 9 of the Trustee Act 1925 provided a further measure of relief for trustees in cases where an excessive amount was advanced. This section provided that the trustee was only liable to make good the sum advanced. Again, the Trustee Act 2000 has repealed this section in respect of mortgages entered into after the coming into force of the 2000 Act. However, after February 2001, if a trustee is accused of advancing an excessive amount on a property that was in other respects a suitable security, a court would assess compensation for breach of trust according to the same principles as set out in section 9. Section 9 merely states what true measure of loss should be in such a case and the same result can be arrived on general principles.

Duty to obtain advice

6.4   After the introduction of the Trustee Act 2000, trustees have an obligation to obtain and consider proper advice before making any investment, unless they reasonably conclude that in all the circumstances it is unnecessary or inappropriate. In general, this will require trustees who are considering making a loan secured on mortgage to obtain the advice of a properly qualified surveyor or valuer. Only if the trustee is himself professionally qualified as a surveyor and the amount of the loan is modest in relation to the property over which the security is being granted would it be prudent to dispense with independent advice.

The process of taking advice requires that the instructions are properly recorded in writing. The valuer ought to be made aware that trust money is proposed to be used as the source of the loan. The trustees should acquaint the valuer with all relevant circumstances of which they are aware. A properly detailed written report should be obtained. The valuer should be asked not only to express a view of the value of the property but should also be asked what amount may safely be advanced and whether he advised that such an advance be made. Ideally, the valuer should be familiar with the local market in which the property is situated or at least have access to information from which he can inform himself as to local conditions and prices. One difficulty that trustees face is that in this litigious age it is extremely common for surveyors and valuers to be reluctant to say more than the bare minimum. Therefore, it may be difficult in practice to get a valuer to provide advice as to what sum may safely be advanced and whether the valuer recommends the particular transaction. Further, valuers nowadays tend to hedge their reports with extensive conditions that are designed to minimise liability on their part. Trustees will need to consider, in any case, whether the exclusion clauses that a valuer attempts to impose are reasonable and capable of being accepted.

The process of making a secured loan also involves obtaining legal advice on the title to be obtained. Trustees should ensure that a properly qualified lawyer is instructed to investigate title and to report on it. Trustees should not really employ the solicitor who acts for the borrower so as to avoid problems with conflicts of interest. In recent years, within the mortgage market, it has become common practice for commercial lenders to employ the borrower's solicitors to investigate and perfect title. This practice, which has itself led to numerous problems such as an increase in mortgage fraud, is not a practice that is consistent with the discharge by trustees of their duty of care and statutory duty to take proper advice.

Trustees are not allowed to lend on mortgage to one of themselves, in the absence of an express power in clear terms (*Fletcher v Green (1864) 33 Beav 426; Stickney v Sewell (1835) 1 Myl & Cr 8*). Trustees are prevented by general principle from engaging in self-dealing and an accommodation by trustees of one of their number by granting a mortgage loan is a classic instance of such a transaction.

The power to make loans

6.5   Trustees cannot make interest-free loans to beneficiaries or, *a fortiori*, third parties unless they have express power to do so. An interest-free loan is obviously not a satisfactory investment. Nowadays, many modern trust instruments do expressly authorise the making of interest-free loans and such loans are often made for tax purposes.

Section 3 of the Trustee Act 2000 empowers trustees to lend on the security of both freehold and leasehold land as 'land' is defined to include any estate or interest in land. The 2000 Act repealed section 8(2) of the Trustee Act 1925 which provided protection from breach of trust to a trustee who lent on the security of leasehold land but did not investigate the lessor's title. Presumably, after February 2001, trustees would be well advised to insist that the freehold title be investigated and proved to their solicitors' satisfaction. Trustees will obviously need to ensure that the terms of the lease offered as security are suitable. The length of the leasehold term and the presence of unusual or onerous covenants are relevant matters to consider.

Conclusion

6.6   The power to invest on mortgage under section 3 of the Trustee Act 2000 is a wide one and would permit investment on equitable mortgages, contributory mortgages or second mortgages. These types of mortgages were prohibited until the introduction of the Trustee Investments Act 1961. After 1961 investments in mortgages of freehold property and leasehold property with 60 years to run were narrow-range investments requiring advice.

However, investment in these types of mortgages requires trustees to tread with a degree of caution since the traditional pre-1961 position was again rooted in common sense. Second mortgages are more vulnerable than first mortgages. Contributory mortgages involve trustees mixing trust money with money belonging to third-party strangers. Equitable mortgages, if protected by registration under the Land Registration Act 2002 or the Land Charges Act 1972, are safe enough. Trustees who are proposing to invest in a mortgage of an unusual character need to obtain proper legal advice on the risks to the trust fund of doing so before proceeding.

Chapter 7

Collective Delegation

Introduction

7.1   The power of an individual trustee to delegate his functions must be distinguished from the power of trustees as a body collectively to delegate. This chapter is concerned with the latter type of delegation since that is the type of delegation that affects trustee investment. The Law Commission in its report Law Com 260 which led to the Trustee Act 2000 stated:

> 'Whilst certain limitations on trustees' powers of delegation are wholly appropriate, others now constitute a serious impediment to the administration of trusts. Trusteeship is an increasingly specialised task that often requires professional skills that the trustees may not have. Far from promoting the more conscientious discharge of the obligations of trusteeship the prohibition on the delegation of fiduciary discretions may force trustees to commit breaches of trust in order to achieve the most effective administration of the trust'.

The old law, in summary, prohibited (in the absence of express authority in the trust instrument) the delegation by trustees of their dispositive powers to distribute the trust property to those entitled to it under the trust, or their fiduciary discretions. The power of selection of trust investments involved the exercise of such a fiduciary discretion. The practical result of categorising powers of investment and certain other powers of management as fiduciary in nature was that many trustees could not employ discretionary fund managers. However, in practice, for any trust that had substantial investments, the employment of a discretionary fund manager was a necessity and this had, in fact, been recognised judicially in *Steel v Wellcome Custodian Trustees Ltd [1988] 1 WLR 167 at 174*. The Law Commission therefore recommended that the old distinction between ministerial acts and fiduciary powers should be abandoned and replaced by a distinction between trustees' powers (i) to administer the trust property, and (ii) their dispositive powers to distribute trust property for the benefit of beneficiaries. The former should be delegable but not the latter. This chapter proposes to explain the old law in more detail and then to state the new law as introduced by the Trustee Act 2000.

The old law

7.2   The fundamental rule was stated authoritatively in the nineteeth-century work, *Sugden on Powers*, in the following terms:

> 'Whenever a power is given . . . if the powers repose a personal trust and confidence in the donee of it to exercise his own judgement and discretion, he cannot refer the power to the execution of another, for *delegatus non potest delegare*'.

The above rule was not absolute and two exceptions reduced its ambit. First, the non-delegation rule merely represented the default position and where the trust instrument expressly provided authority to do so, a trustee was free to delegate his or her powers. Secondly, the rule only prohibited delegation of their dispositive powers or fiduciary discretions. These included the selection of investments (*Rowland v Witherden (1851) 3 Mac & G 568, 574) and the decision whether or not to sell or lease trust property (Clarke v The Royal Panopticon (1857) 4 Drew 26 at 29; Robson v Flight (1865) 4 De GJ & Sm 608*).

The rule did not, therefore, preclude the delegation by trustees of ministerial acts. By ministerial acts one means those acts which implement a decision after trustees have exercised their discretionary powers by making the decision as to what is to be done. The dividing line between fiduciary discretions and ministerial powers is, however, not clearly defined and attempts to define the boundary in the United States have been unsuccessful.

Meaning of section 23

7.3   After 1926, the default power which applied in the absence of any express power in the trust instrument was found in section 23 of the Trustee Act 1925. The powers in that section applied in addition to any powers contained in the trust instrument and only if and so far as no contrary intention was expressed in that trust instrument. Settlors could add to, vary or exclude the statutory power (Trustee Act 1925, s 69(2)).

Section 23(1) provided:

> 'Trustees or personal representatives may, instead of acting personally, employ and pay an agent, whether a solicitor, banker, stockbroker, or other person to transact any business or act required to be transacted or done in the execution of the trust, or the administration of the testator's or intestate's estate, including the receipt and payment of capital money and shall be entitled to be allowed and paid all charges and expenses so incurred and shall not be responsible for the default of any such agent if employed in good faith'.

The leading case on the meaning of section 23 is *Re Vickery [1931] 1 Ch 572*. In that case, Maugham J held that section 23(1) had abolished the old common law rule that provided that trustees could only delegate their functions in cases of moral necessity. Section 23, however, only authorised the delegation of ministerial functions and not fiduciary discretions. This is readily apparent when one compares subsection (1) with subsection (2), which is the section that governed delegation in respect of trust property situated outside the United Kingdom. That subsection did enable delegation of discretionary powers in relation to such foreign property. Nor did section 23(1) enable sub-delegation by an agent. Section 23(1) stated that trustees can only delegate acts which are required to be transacted or done in the execution of the trust. There was doubt whether the subsection allowed trustees to delegate functions to an agent on general retainer. Arguably, the subsection only allowed the delegation of specific acts or particular business.

Good faith

7.4   Because under section 23(1) trustees were not responsible for the defaults of agents if employed in good faith, it was thought that provided they acted in good faith, trustees could employ agents on the basis that they would not be liable for acts of negligence committed in the execution of the agency (see the view expressed in Appendix C to Law Com 260).

However, in *Re Weall (1889) 42 Ch D 674*, Kekewich J said that trustees had to consider carefully the terms on which they employed agents and could not simply accept without question the conditions that they were offered. The position was consequently unclear. More controversial still was the question whether trustees had power to authorise agents to engage in conduct which the trustees could not. The better view was that section 23(1), being a default power, did so enable them. This point is particularly relevant to investment managers and discretionary fund managers as the standard terms on which such agents act may include a liberty to buy or sell from the trust and to keep any incidental profits from their employment.

Practical issues

7.5   Section 23(3) of the Trustee Act 1925 re-enacted with amendments a number of earlier statutory provisions that were aimed at specific practical problems. Section 23(3)(a) dealt with trustees selling land and authorised them to appoint a solicitor as agent to receive and give a discharge for any money or valuable consideration or property receivable by the trustees under the trust by permitting the trustee to have custody of and produce a deed containing a receipt for such money or valuable consideration. Section 23(3)(c) provided that a trustee may appoint a banker or solicitor to be his agent to receive and give a discharge for any money payable to the trustees under or by virtue of any policy of insurance by permitting the banker or solicitor to have custody of and to produce the policy of insurance with a receipt signed by the trustee.

Standard of care

7.6   The standard of care that applied in the appointment of an agent, that applied pre-1925, was that of reasonable prudence. Trustees were expected to act with reasonable prudence both when appointing agents and in negotiating the terms on which the agent was employed (*Re Weall (1889) 42 Ch D 674; Speight v Gaunt (1883) 9 App Cas 1*). After 1925 four subsections applied to govern the position, namely section 23(1)–(3) and section 30(1) of the Trustee Act 1925. These sections did not, however, interrelate in a coherent fashion and the law was left in a state of unsatisfactory uncertainty.

Re Vickery [1931] 1 Ch 572 is the leading authority on the interpretation of the above provisions. In that case, a sole executor employed a solicitor to wind up the testator's estate and authorised him to get in certain sums of money. The executor was then informed by one of the beneficiaries that the solicitor was not to be trusted and he was asked to use another solicitor. As the solicitor was then promising to finally settle the matter, the executor left matters in his hands. The solicitor absconded and the money that had been in his hands for over a month was lost. An action for breach of duty was brought. It was held that the executor was not liable.

Propositions derived from Re Vickery

7.7   Four propositions can be derived from the authority as follows.

1.   Given the terms of section 23(1), trustees were not liable for loss due to the appointment of an agent provided that they had acted in good faith. This proposition was criticised because it meant that trustees who honestly but negligently delegated some functions to an incompetent or dishonest agent escaped liability. Be that as it may, the literal subjective approach taken in *Re Vickery* was endorsed in the modern case of *Steel v Wellcome Custodian Trustees Ltd [1988] 1 WLR 167 at 174*.

2.   The proviso to section 23(3) had no application to delegations made under subsection (1). The proviso to subsection (3) stated that a trustee should not be exempt if he permitted money, valuable consideration or property to remain in the hands of a banker or solicitor for longer than was reasonably necessary to enable the banker or solicitor to pay or transfer the same to the trustee.

        The protection afforded by section 23(1) therefore was not spent once the appointment was made but continued thereafter and applied to the supervision of the agent once appointed. The effect of this was that subsection (3) was apparently superfluous because the power to delegate in subsection (1) was wide enough to encompass the specific powers of delegation set down in subsection (3). If the former power was not subject to the proviso which applied to subsection (3) then trustees would always choose to delegate by using their power under subsection (1).

3.   The statutory indemnity in section 30(1) of the Trustee Act 1925 did not apply to protect a trustee in all cases where the trust had suffered loss. That section provided as follows:

'A trustee shall be chargeable only for the money and securities actually received by him notwithstanding his signing any receipt for the sake of conformity, and shall be answerable and accountable only for his own acts, receipts, neglects or defaults and not for those of any other trustee, nor any banker, broker, or other person with whom any trust money or securities may be deposited, nor for the insufficiency or deficiency of any securities, nor for any other loss unless the same happens through his own wilful default'.

The protection of this section was said in *Re Vickery* to apply only to losses which arose from:

- a trustee signing receipts for the sake of conformity;
- the wrongful acts or defaults of another trustee;
- the wrongful acts or defaults of a banker, broker or other agent with whom trust money or securities had been deposited;
- the insufficiency or deficiency of securities; or
- any analogous loss.

4.   The phrase 'wilful default' in section 30(1) had the meaning given to it in *Re City Equitable Fire Insurance Co Ltd [1925] Ch 407*, namely either a consciousness of negligence or breach of duty, or a recklessness in the performance of a duty. Maugham J's interpretation of the phrase in *Re Vickery* was controversial in that it was contrary to earlier authority which held that those words meant no more than 'breach of duty' but it also set the obligations of trustees at a much lower level than had applied before and one that was arguably inappropriate. It was also not obvious why in relation to the five types of loss identified in point 3 above, a lower standard of care was expected of trustees than in relation to other acts and omissions. Maugham J's interpretation in *Re Vickery* was, however, endorsed by the Court of Appeal in the case of *Armitage v Nurse [1998] Ch 241 at 252* where Millett LJ stated that in the context of a trustee's exclusion clause, such as section 30 of the Law of Property Act 1925, wilful default meant a deliberate breach of trust.

The new law under the Trustee Act 2000

7.8   Subsections (1) and (2) of section 11 of the Trustee Act 2000 provide as follows:

'(1) Subject to the provisions of this Part, the trustees of a trust may authorise any person to exercise any or all of their delegable functions as their agent.

(2) In the case of a trust other than a charitable trust, the trustees' delegable functions consist of any function other than—

(a)   any function relating to whether or in what way any assets of the trust should be distributed,

(b)   any power to decide whether any fees or other payment due to be made out of the trust funds should be made out of income or capital,

(c)   any power to appoint a person to be a trustee of the trust, or

(d)   any power conferred by any other enactment or the trust instrument which permits the trustees to delegate any of their functions or to appoint a person to act as a nominee or custodian.'

Power to appoint agents

7.9   The new power to appoint agents is in addition to the powers conferred on trustees otherwise than by the Trustee Act 2000 but it may be restricted or excluded by the trust instrument or by legislation (Trustee Act 2000, s 26). One question that arises is whether the common law powers that existed prior to the introduction of the Trustee Act 1925 are available. For instance, section 23(2) of the Trustee Act 1925 which governed the appointment of agents in connection with trust of foreign property was repealed by the Trustee Act 2000. However, that section was itself declaratory of the common law in so far as it permitted delegation of trust discretions, both administrative and dispositive affecting foreign property (see *Stuart v Norton (1860) 14 Moo PCC 17*). Because the Trustee Act 2000 does not permit delegation of dispositive functions, the survival of the old common law power would be of some significance. However, the Law Commission clearly did not intend the common law powers to survive – see Law Com no 260 at para 4.13 where the Commission stated that it was no longer justifiable to have an exception for foreign property. The reason behind the exception was slow communication with foreign countries in past times. Now that communication is instantaneous the exception was thought unnecessary by the Law Commission. In the author's view, the common law powers will not have survived the enactment of section 23(2) of the Trustee Act 1925 and, if that section is itself replaced, the old powers should not spring back to life. For a contrary view see *Lewin on Trusts* at para 36–10C.

Agents

7.10   The statutory duty of care will apply to a trustee when entering into arrangements under which a person is authorised under section 11 or under any other power, however conferred, to exercise functions as an agent (see sections 1 and 2 and Schedule 1, paras 3(1)(a) and (d)). The duty also applies to the review of agents (para 3(1)(e)). Paragraph 3(2) provides that, for the purposes of paragraph 3(1), entering into arrangements under which a person is authorised to exercise functions as an agent includes selecting the person who is to act and determining any terms on which he is to act.

However, the initial decision whether or not to delegate does not seem to be subject to the statutory duty. Given that section 23(1) of the Trustee Act 1925 was held in *Re Vickery* to have revolutionised the law on delegation, enabling trustees to delegate whether there was a necessity or not, it would have been odd for the 2000 Act to have subjected the decision of trustees whether to delegate to a duty of care (see *[1931] 1 Ch 572 at 581*). Once the decision to delegate has been taken, the duty of care cuts in and a trustee is bound to be judicious in his selection of the agent.

Dispositive powers cannot be delegated

7.11   Section 11(2)(a) provides that trustees cannot delegate their dispositive powers, ie their power to determine whether to distribute trust property and to which trust beneficiaries. This provision applies only to powers of distribution and would not extend to a decision to sell a trust asset to a third party or to exercise a right of indemnity over it. The provision would cover:

- powers of appointment;
- powers of advancement;
- powers of maintenance; and
- powers of revocation of interests.

It is not obvious whether a power of appropriation between two or more funds is within the exclusion or not since the exercise of such a power may have serious consequences for a beneficiary in that the type of property appropriated in satisfaction may radically affect the income and also the ultimate capital entitlement of a beneficiary.

Fees and expenses

7.12   Section 11(2)(b) excludes any power to decide whether fees or other payments due to be made out of the trust funds should be made out of capital or income. Generally, the allocation of expenses between income and capital is a matter of right and not a matter of discretion, but it is common for trust instruments to contain express powers that confer a discretion on trustees to make such a determination. Obviously, the provision prevents the unattractive possibility of an agent determining how his own fees should be paid. The exclusion in this provision means that all questions in relation to fees are kept under the direct control of the trustees.

Appointing new trustees

7.13   Section 11(2)(c) excludes powers of appointment of new trustees. Again, the power to appoint a new trustee is of great importance and the power has traditionally been categorised as fiduciary in nature (*Re Skeats' Settlement (1889) 42 Ch D 522 at 526*).

Sub-delegation

7.14   Section 11(2)(d) excludes any power conferred by any other enactment or the trust instrument which permits trustees to delegate any of their
functions or to appoint a person to act as a nominee or a custodian. This is aimed
at preventing sub-delegation by prohibiting trustees from delegating any power
to delegate that they may have under the trust instrument or under any other Act.

The drafting is possibly defective if its intention was to prohibit all form of
sub-delegation since nothing in the wording of section 11 would seem to
preclude trustees from delegating their statutory power to appoint agents. The
Law Commission in its report recognised that trustees did need to be able to
delegate on terms that permitted sub-delegation because if trustees wanted to
employ discretionary fund managers they would often be forced to employ such
a person on the person's standard terms which would include a term permitting
sub-delegation.

The Law Commission recommended that a power to employ sub-agents should
be conferred by the new proposed Act but subject to the condition that trustees
should only be permitted to do so in cases where it was 'reasonably necessary'.
However, section 14(2) and (3) of the Trustee Act 2000, which imposes such a
condition, refers in subsection (3)(a) to a term permitting the agent to appoint a
substitute. A substitute is not the same as a sub-agent. The draft Act annexed to
the Law Commission report employed the same words as enacted in the Act and
it may be that an error of drafting crept in and was never tackled as the Act made
its progress through Parliament.

Under section 12, trustees may appoint as their agent one or more of their
number. Trustees may not authorise two or more persons to exercise the same
function unless they are to exercise it jointly. A beneficiary may not be
appointed an agent even if the beneficiary is also a trustee. A person may act as
an agent even if he has also been appointed as a nominee or custodian under
section 16, 17 or 18 or any other power.

Subject to the terms of section 12, trustees may appoint any person as their agent
but they are subject to the statutory duty of care in making such an appointment
and are therefore bound to choose a properly qualified and upright person to act.

Choice of agent

7.15   Trustees appointing agents are bound to exercise the statutory duty of
care. Prior to 1926 and the introduction of section 23(1) of the Trustee Act 1925,
which imposed a test of 'good faith', trustees were subject to a duty to exercise
proper care in their appointment. The Trustee Act 2000 reimposed a similar test.
A number of old cases illustrate the principle and are relevant to the application
of section 11 of the 2000 Act.

Duty of care

7.16   In *Budge v Gummow (1872) 7 Ch App 719*, trustees were charged with breach of trust arising out of an advance of trust money on the security of a hotel in Broadstairs. The security proved to be grossly insufficient. The advance was made on the basis of a surveyor's report that over-valued the hotel. James LJ held that the surveyor's report was one upon which no sensible or prudent man would ever lend such a sum as that advanced. The fact that the surveyor was based in London and a stranger to Broadstairs meant that he was unable to estimate the value of the hotel licence and there was no basis for the value put upon the licence by the surveyor.

In *Fry v Tapson (1884) 28 Ch D 268,* trustees who had power to lend on mortgage advanced a sum of £5,000 on property in Liverpool. The trustees did not exercise their own judgement as to the choice of a valuer but accepted the suggestion of their solicitors that a London surveyor who had introduced the security to them, and was in fact the agent of the mortgagor with a pecuniary interest in the completion of the mortgage, should value the property. The valuation report over-valued the property and the mortgagor became bankrupt. The trustees were found liable for the loss. Kay J found that the trustees should not have employed or relied on the report of the valuer. He was a London valuer with no local knowledge and his employment was inexpedient for that reason alone. The fact that he was employed by the mortgagor and had an interest in the transaction only made matters worse. The rule that trustees were not liable for the default of their agents was subject to the limitation that the agent should not be employed out of the ordinary scope of his business.

In *Re Weall (1889) 42 Ch D 674* trustees of a will trust employed a solicitor to collect rents due and allowed him to deduct from the rents certain costs including his own fees. The tenant for life objected and brought an action alleging that some of the costs were chargeable against capital and not out of income. The court held that a trustee was entitled to employ a solicitor and, as long as he selected a properly qualified one, he was not responsible for that agent's intelligence or honesty. However, he could not entrust the agent with any duties which the agent was willing to undertake or pay him any remuneration which he might demand. The trustee was bound to exercise his discretion on both these points. The court on the facts held that if the solicitor had not been allowed to receive the rent and consequently the means of paying himself, the dispute would never have arisen.

In *Robinson v Harkin [1896] 2 Ch 415*, trustees entrusted the whole of a trust fund to an outside stockbroker, ie a stockbroker who was not a member of the Stock Exchange. The stockbroker was not a man of any great reputation and misapplied part of the trust fund for his own use. The trustees were held liable on the grounds that they had not exercised proper care in the selection of the broker.

From the above cases the following propositions can be derived:

- the agent should be properly qualified to perform the task entrusted to him;

- the agent must be employed to act within the usual scope of such an agent;

- the agent must be of good repute and standing in his course of business;

- the agent must be independent and not have an interest that is adverse or potentially adverse to that of the trust.

Terms of engagement

7.17   In agreeing the terms of engagement of an agent, trustees are subject to the statutory duty of care. Section 14(1) provides that the trustees may authorise a person to exercise functions as their agent on such terms as to remuneration and other matters as they may determine. Section 14(2) goes on to provide that trustees may not authorise a person to exercise functions as their agent on any of the terms mentioned in subsection (3) unless it is reasonably necessary for them to do so.

The terms set out in subsection (3) are:

(a)   a term permitting the agent to appoint a substitute;

(b)   a term restricting the liability of the agent or his substitute to the trustees or any beneficiary;

(c)   a term permitting the agent to act in circumstances capable of giving rise to a conflict of interest.

Paragraph (a) above applies to the case where an agent appoints a substitute for himself. As noted at 7.14 above, the Law Commission report at para 4.25 and 4.26 considered that trustees ought to be able to sub-delegate provided that it was reasonably necessary for them to do so. The use of the word 'substitute' was presumably aimed at the situation of sub-delegation but the choice of the term 'substitute' suggests a person who replaces the agent rather than someone who acts under him.

Paragraph (b) is a recognition of modern commercial reality. Nowadays many large reputable investment managers and discretionary fund managers will only agree to act on their standard terms which will inevitably contain exclusion clauses restricting the agent's liability. It is therefore pragmatic and sensible that trustees have power to enter into arrangements that contain exclusion clauses, if this cannot be avoided. The same rationale lies behind paragraph (c). Again, the Law Commission recognised that there may be circumstances where trustees have no practical choice but to authorise agents to act in circumstances capable of giving rise to conflicts of interest.

The Law Commission recognised all of the above situations as being undesir-able but necessary evils in the modern world of trust administration. Trustees ought not to enter into such arrangements casually and serious consideration will need to be given by them to the question whether it is reasonably necessary to enter into those arrangements on the terms mentioned in section 14(3). Trustees will be wise to properly record the basis of their decisions and the reason why they felt it was necessary to sanction the particular arrangements.

Linked functions

7.18   Section 13 of the Trustee Act 2000 provides that a person who is authorised under section 11 to exercise a function is (whatever the terms of the agency) subject to any specific duties or restrictions attached to the function. For example, a person who is authorised to exercise the general power of investment is subject to the duties under section 4 (the standard investment criteria) in relation to that power. A person who is authorised to exercise a power under section 11, which is subject to a requirement to take advice, is not subject to the requirement if he is the kind of person from whom it would have been proper for the trustees, in compliance with the requirement, to obtain advice (subs (2)).

Subsections (4) and (5) apply to a trust to which section 11(1) of the Trusts of Land and Appointment of Trustees Act 1996 applies (subs (3)). That section imposes a duty on trustees to consult beneficiaries and to give effect to their wishes.

Section 13(4) of the Trustee Act 2000 provides that trustees may not appoint an agent on terms that prevent them from complying with section 11 of the 1996 Act. Section 13(5) provides that:

> 'A person who is authorised under section 11 to exercise any function relating to land subject to the trust is not subject to section 11(1) of the 1996 Act'.

Section 13 applies only to a delegation under the statutory power in section 11. Agents are not subject to the statutory duty of care under section 1 of the Trustee Act 2000 but are made subject to the specific duties attached to a particular function such as the requirement to have regard to the standard investment criteria and to take advice.

Section 13(4) and (5) make it clear that the duty to consult beneficiaries that is imposed by section 11 of the Trusts of Land and Appointment of Trustees Act 1996 may not be delegated. Trustees have to exercise this duty themselves and they may not delegate on terms that prevent them from discharging this duty.

Asset management

7.19   'Asset management functions' are defined in section 15(5) as the trustees' functions in relation to:

(a)   the investment of assets subject to the trust,

(b)   the acquisition of property which is to be subject to the trust, and

(c)   managing property which is subject to the trust and disposing of, or creating or disposing of an interest in, such property.

Section 15(1) of the Trustee Act 2000 provides that trustees may not authorise a person to exercise any of their asset management functions as their agent except by an agreement which is in writing or evidenced in writing. Section 15(2) states that trustees may not authorise an agent to exercise asset management functions unless they have prepared a policy statement that gives guidance as to how the functions should be exercised. The agreement under which the agent is to act must include a term to the effect that the agent will secure compliance with the policy statement or any revised statement if the statement is reviewed under section 22 of the Act. Section 15(3) requires the trustees to formulate any guidance given in the policy statement with a view to ensuring that the functions will be exercised in the best interests of the trust. Under section 15(4) the policy statement has to be in writing or evidenced in writing.

Policy statement

7.20   A policy statement under section 15 in relation to investment should typically provide guidance as to the following matters:

- the balance to be struck between income and capital;

- the degree of risk to be undertaken in the choice of investments;

- diversity – particularly if the trust receives a dominant holding in a private company;

- the degree of liquidity;

- any ethical considerations;

- the proportion of property to be invested in foreign investments (if any);

- attitude to foreign currency exposure;

- base currency in the case of trusts of foreign property;

- specific investments that may not be sold;

- specific investments that may not be acquired, eg shares in a company that competes with a family company;

- frequency of valuations and method of reporting information to the trustees.

A precedent of a policy statement can be found in APPENDIX 1. A policy statement in relation to the acquisition of land should deal with the type of property that can be acquired, the value of it, and the quality of title required to be obtained. It could also specify the sort of terms on which land could be sold, let or charged.

Section 22 deals with the review of agents, nominees and custodians. It provides that while an agent continues to act for the trust the trustees must keep under review the arrangements under which the agent acts and how those arrangements are being put into effect. They must consider whether or not to intervene and must intervene if they decide that there is a need to do so.

In the case of agents exercising asset management functions, section 22(2) provides expressly that trustees must consider whether there is a need to revise or replace the policy statement made under section 15. If they decide that there is such a need they must act on their decision. They also have a duty to assess whether the policy statement is being complied with. Section 15(3)–(5) apply to a revised or replacement policy statement as they apply to the making of the original statement. The new statement must therefore provide the appropriate guidance and be in writing or evidenced in writing.

Liability of trustees

7.21   Section 23(1) of the Trustee Act 2000 provides that a trustee is not liable for any act or default of an agent, nominee or custodian unless he has failed to comply with the duty of care applicable to him under paragraph 3 of Schedule 1 when entering into the arrangements under which the person acts as agent, nominee or custodian or when carrying out his duties under section 22 (ie review of arrangements). Schedule 1, para 3(2) makes it clear that entering into the arrangements under which a person is authorised to exercise functions as an agent includes in particular:

(a)   selecting the person who is to act,

(b)   determining any terms on which he is to act, and

(c)   if the person is being authorised to exercise asset management functions, the preparation of a policy statement under section 15.

It is important to remember that section 23 is an exoneration clause and not a clause imposing liability. Therefore, a trustee could still argue that his own breach has not caused the loss complained of. The liability of a trustee springs from breach by the trustee of a duty.

If an agent is the source of a loss to the trust, the trustee will escape liability unless he himself is at fault in the ways specified in section 23. Thus the trustee will be liable if he:

•   was negligent in his choice of agent;

•   was negligent in setting the terms of the agent or the terms of a section 15 policy statement;

•   failed to supervise the agent properly; or

•   failed to review the terms under which the agent acts.

Section 23(2) provides that if a trustee has agreed to a term under which the agent, nominee or custodian is permitted to appoint a substitute, the trustee is not liable for any act or default of the substitute unless he has failed to comply with the duty of care applicable to him under paragraph 3 of Schedule 1 when agreeing that term or when carrying out his duties under section 22 in so far as they relate to the use of the substitute.

Section 23 of the Trustee Act 2000 provides a much lesser degree of protection to trustees than the old sections 23(1) and 30 of the Trustee Act 1925. Under those sections as interpreted in *Re Vickery [1931] Ch 572*, trustees were protected in respect of the defaults of agents provided that the agents had been appointed in good faith. It was really only the appointment that mattered. Under section 30, liability required conscious breach of duty or recklessness. Section 23 of the new Act only confers protection on trustees if they have complied with their duties in connection with the appointment, supervision and review of agents. Trustees, therefore, only obtain protection if they meet a much higher standard than under the old law.

Section 24 of the Trustee Act 2000 provides that a failure by the trustees to act within the limits of the powers conferred by Part IV of the Act in authorising an agent does not invalidate the appointment. This provides protection to third parties dealing with such agents and means that transactions effected by the agent are not void or defective by reason of the manner of the agent's appointment.

Remuneration of agents

7.22   Section 32 of the Trustee Act 2000 deals with remuneration of agents appointed under the Act or under any other statutory power or under any express power in the trust instrument.

Trustees may remunerate an agent if he is engaged on terms entitling him to be remunerated for those services and the amount does not exceed such remuneration as is reasonable in the circumstances for the provision of those services by him or on behalf of the trust. The trustees may reimburse the agent out of the trust funds for any expenses properly incurred by him in exercising his functions as an agent. If trustees commit themselves by contract to pay sums in excess of what is reasonable or do, in practice, pay excessive sums, then they are personally liable for the excess.

Chapter 8

Nominees and Custodians

The old law

8.1   At common law, trustees were subject to a duty to take such steps as were reasonable to secure control of the trust property and to keep control of it (*Wyman v Paterson [1900] AC 271*). One concomitant of this rule was that trustees could not make an investment jointly with one or more other persons (*Webb v Jonas (1888) 39 Ch D 660*). Where there were two or more trustees, it was their duty to ensure that title to the trust property was vested in their joint names so that it could be transferred only with the consent of all the trustees (*Re Flower and the Metropolitan Board of Works (1884) 27 Ch D 592*). The documents relating to the trust property could, however, remain in the custody of just one of the trustees (*Cottam v Eastern Counties Railway Co (1860) 1 J & H 243*). Therefore, in the absence of an express power in the trust instrument or in statute, trustees could not vest property in nominees nor place trust documents in the hands of a custodian without committing a breach of trust.

Section 21 of the Trustee Act 1925 gave trustees a power to deposit documents relating to the trust with any banker or banking company or other company whose business included the undertaking of the safe custody of documents. Section 7(1) of the Trustee Act 1925 imposed a duty on trustees to deposit bearer securities with a banker or banking company for the purposes of safe custody and the collection of income. Section 4 of the Public Trustee Act 1906 conferred a power to appoint the Public Trustee or certain other bodies corporate to act as custodian trustees.

The Law Commission considered that the old law was unduly restrictive to meet the needs of modern trustees. In particular, the law did not enable trustees to use nominees to provide an administrative service in relation to investments, to facilitate dealings by a discretionary fund manager, as one method of using the CREST system (see 1.3 above), in relation to overseas investments that were traded using a computerised clearing system or where registered land was held in trust to avoid the need for regular changes in the register when trustees changed.

The new law: Trustee Act 2000

Nominees

8.2   Section 16 of the Trustee Act 2000 provides the power to appoint nominees. Under section 16(1) trustees may appoint a person to act as their nominee in relation to such of the assets of the trust as they determine (other than settled land) and take such steps as are necessary to ensure that those assets are vested in a person so appointed. An appointment under section 16 must be in writing or evidenced in writing. Section 16 does not apply to any trust having a custodian trustee or in relation to any assets vested in the official custodian for charities.

The term 'nominee' is not defined in the Act. However, in the context in which the term is used it clearly means a person in whom title to property is vested and who is bound to deal with it as the trustees may direct. The statutory power applies to existing trusts and is in addition to any power conferred otherwise than by the 2000 Act but can be restricted or excluded by the trust instrument (Trustee Act 2000, s 26).

Custodians

8.3   Section 17 provides the power to appoint a custodian. Section 17(2) provides that a person is a custodian in relation to assets if he undertakes the safe custody of the assets or of any documents or records concerning the assets. The appointment must be in writing or evidenced in writing. Again the section does not apply to any trust having a custodian trustee or in relation to any assets vested in the official custodian for charities. The statutory power is additional to any power conferred otherwise than by the Act but may be restricted or excluded by the trust instrument.

Section 18(1) of the Trustee Act 2000 provides that if trustees retain or invest in bearer securities they must appoint a person to act as custodian of those securities. Subsection (2) provides that the above obligation does not apply if the trust instrument or any enactment or provision in subordinate legislation permits the trustees to retain or invest in bearer securities without appointing a person to act as custodian.

Duty of care

8.4   The statutory duty of care applies to trustees entering into arrange-ments under which a person is to act as nominee or custodian (see Trustee Act 2000, ss 1, 2 and Sch 1, para 3). The duty applies to the selection of the person appointed and the fixing of the terms on which he is to act.

Section 19 contains conditions applicable to the appointment of nominees or custodians.

Section 19(1) states that a person may not be appointed as a nominee or custodian under section 16, 17 or 18 unless one of the relevant conditions is satisfied. The relevant conditions are that the person:

- carries on business which consists of or includes acting as a nominee or custodian;

- is a body corporate which is controlled by the trustees;

- is a body corporate recognised under section 9 of the Administration of Justice Act 1985.

The test set out in section 840 of the Income and Corporation Taxes Act 1988 is applied to determine whether a body corporate is controlled by the trustees (subsection (3)). Charitable trustees must act in accordance with guidance given by the Charity Commissioners concerning the selection for appointment as a nominee or custodian (subsection (4)).

The persons whom the trustees may appoint under section 16, 17 or 18 include one of their own number if that one is a trust corporation, or two (or more) of their number if they are to act as joint nominees or joint custodians.

Persons may act as both nominee and custodian

8.5   Section 19(6) provides that a person may be appointed by trustees to act as their nominee even though he is also appointed to act as their custodian or authorised to act as their agent under section 11 or any other power. In the same way a person may be appointed to act as a custodian even though he is also acting as nominee or agent.

Terms of appointment

8.6   Section 20 provides that trustees may appoint nominees or custodians on such terms as to remuneration and other matters as they may determine. This is subject to sections 29 to 32. Section 20(2) provides, however, that trustees may not appoint nominees or custodians on certain terms unless it is reasonably necessary for them to do so. The certain terms are set out in subsection (3) and are:

(a)   a term permitting the nominee or custodian to appoint a substitute;

(b)   a term restricting the liability of the nominee or custodian or his substitute to the trustees or to any beneficiary;

(c)   a term permitting the nominee or custodian to act in circumstances capable of giving rise to a conflict of interest.

Subsections (2) and (3) of section 20 mirror section 14(2) and (3) in relation to agents. The provision is a pragmatic recognition of the commercial realities that apply in the present market. Many professional organisations offering services as nominees and custodians will only act in accordance with their own contractual terms and these will often include clauses of the nature addressed in section 20(3).

Section 21 provides that section 22 (review of agents, nominees and custodians) and section 23 (liability for defaults of agents, nominees and custodians) apply in a case where trustees have authorised an agent or appointed a nominee or custodian under the statutory powers in the Trustee Act 2000. Sections 22 and 23 also apply in a case where trustees have authorised an agent or appointed a nominee or custodian by using an express power or a power conferred by another statute or statutory instrument. However, if the application of sections 22 and 23 is inconsistent with the terms of the trust instrument or the enactment or provision of subordinate legislation, the section in question does not apply.

The duty to review

8.7   Section 22, as we have seen in connection with agents, imposes duties to keep under review the arrangements under which an agent, nominee or custodian acts and how these arrangements are being put into effect. There is, therefore, a duty to consider whether the arrangements as agreed are satisfactory but also to scrutinise whether the agreed terms are being carried out. Trustees must also consider whether to exercise any power of intervention and, if they decide that there is a need to exercise such a power, they must act on their decision (section 22(1)(b) and (c)). A power of intervention is defined in subsection (4) as including a power to give directions to the agent, nominee or custodian or a power to revoke the authorisation or appointment.

Remuneration

8.8   Section 32 governs remuneration of nominees and custodians as well as agents. The section applies whether the nominee or custodian is appointed under the statutory powers in the Trustee Act 2000 or by an express power in the trust instrument or by some other statutory power. Trustees may remunerate nominees and custodians if they have been engaged on terms entitling them to remuneration and the amount does not exceed such remuneration as is reasonable in the circumstances for the provision of the relevant services. Expenses that are properly incurred by the nominee or custodian may be reimbursed out of the trust fund under section 32(3). Trustees who pay unreasonably excessive remuneration are personally liable for the excess over the reasonable amount.

Section 32 does not apply to a trustee who has been appointed as a nominee or custodian.

Liability

8.9   Section 23 of the Trustee Act 2000 (which was discussed at 7.21 above in relation to agents), provides a degree of protection for trustees in respect of the defaults of nominees or custodians. The protection requires the trustees to comply with the duty of care applicable under paragraph 3 of Schedule 1 when entering into arrangements and when carrying out a review under section 22. If a trustee has agreed to a term whereby a nominee or custodian can appoint a substitute the trustee is not liable for any act or default of the substitute unless he has failed to comply with the duty of care applicable to him under paragraph 3 of Schedule 1 when agreeing to the term or when carrying out his duties of review under section 22 in so far as they relate to the use of the substitute.

Section 23, as noted above, is an exoneration provision and does not impose liability. Another point to appreciate is that the validity of an appointment of an agent or nominee would not be affected by a breach by a trustee of his duty of care in connection with the arrangements for the appointment.

Section 24 provides that a failure by trustees to act within the limits of their powers conferred by Part IV of the Act in authorising agents or appointing nominees or custodians does not invalidate the appointment. Therefore, third parties dealing with the agent or nominee or custodian need not worry about whether or not the appointment has been made in compliance with the trustees' powers.

Chapter 9

The Old Law: Trustee Investments Act 1961

Status of the Trustee Investments Act 1961

9.1   Before the Trustee Act 2000 came into force on 1 February 2001, trustees' investment functions were regulated by the Trustee Investments Act 1961. That Act was repealed upon the coming into force of the Trustee Act 2000 (section 40(3), Sch 4, Part I). Further, the part of the new Act dealing with investment, Part II, is expressed by section 7(1) to apply to trusts whether created before or after the Act's commencement. The 1961 Act will, therefore, not be relevant in relation to any future exercise by trustees of their investment functions. However, it will nevertheless remain significant for some years since the propriety of past investments (or non-investments) by trustees will have to be considered in the context of the legislation prevailing at the time the investment was made. Accordingly, if beneficiaries alleged that a trustee had invested in an unauthorised manner in 2000 and had thereby caused the trust fund to suffer loss, the question whether the investment in question was indeed unauthorised would be considered by reference to the 1961 Act.

Overview and history of the Trustee Investments Act 1961

The law before the Trustee Investments Act 1961

9.2   When it was enacted, the Trustee Investments Act 1961 represented a considerable advance on the previous law regulating trustee investment functions. Under section 1 of the Trustee Act 1925, trustees were permitted to invest only in certain specified types of security. This 'statutory list' was highly restrictive in nature and consisted largely of securities which yielded interest at a fixed rate and were repayable at par. In particular, trustees were not permitted to invest in equities of any sort. The justification for this was that such investment is inherently speculative and so carries a risk that the value of the trust capital will fall. While this ensured that the nominal capital value of the trust fund would not decrease, inflation caused their value to fall in real terms. By the 1950s the restrictive approach to investment embodied in the Trustee Act 1925 was seen as outdated and as serving to benefit neither income nor capital beneficiaries; in 1952 the Nathan Committee recommended reform of the law.

The view that the powers conferred by the 1925 Act were inadequate, at least in relation to some trusts, extended to the courts. In *Re Royal Society's Charitable Trusts [1956] Ch 87* it was held that the court had power to extend the powers of charitable trustees by virtue of the special position obtaining in the law of charities. In *Re Brassey's Settlement [1955] 1 WLR 192*, the court was prepared to extend the powers of investment of non-charitable trustees under section 57 of the Trustee Act 1925, which confers on the court power to authorise dealings with trust property which are not permitted by the trust instrument. Following the coming into force of the Variation of Trusts Act 1958, similar applications were made under that Act, although it has since been held (in *Anker-Petersen v Anker-Petersen (1991) 16 LS Gaz 32*) that applications asking for trustees' investment powers to be extended should after all be made under section 57 of the Trustee Act 1925 unless it is also intended that the beneficial interests under the trusts are to be varied.

Structure of the Trustee Investments Act 1961

9.3   Given this background, it is unsurprising that the principal innovation made by the Trustee Investments Act 1961 was to permit trustees to invest in a much broader range of investments including equities. However, it was still felt necessary to strike a balance between allowing trustees to take advantage of the available investment opportunities so as to achieve satisfactory income production on the one hand, and ensuring that the capital of the fund would be adequately protected on the other. This was to be achieved by providing that if trustees wished to invest in what were called 'wider-range investments', meaning specified investments of a more speculative nature than those previously permitted, they would have to divide the fund into two equal parts (later the fund was to be divided in the proportions 3:1, the larger part being the wider-range part).

The 'narrower-range part' was then to be invested exclusively in corresponding 'narrower-range investments', while the wider-range part could be invested entirely in wider-range investments or in some combination of wider-range and narrower-range investments as the trustees saw fit.

Criticisms of the Trustee Investments Act 1961

9.4   In time, however, the powers conferred by the 1961 Act itself came themselves to be regarded as inadequate. Three common criticisms were identified in the Law Commission Report which preceded the enactment of the Trustee Act 2000 (see Law Com. no. 260 'Trustees' Powers and Duties' at paragraph 2.17).

First, the requirement that the trust fund be divided into two parts, and the mechanism for ensuring that a sufficient proportion of the fund remained invested in narrower-range investments, was described as a 'crude and administratively burdensome attempt to regulate the degree of risk to which trustees may expose the trust'.

Secondly, the list of wider-range investments set out in the 1961 Act was seen as too restrictive. For example, trustees were only permitted to invest in equities which met somewhat stringent conditions. Under Schedule 1, Part IV, para 3, investment was only permitted in companies:

- with total issued and paid up share capital of at least one million pounds; and

- which had in each of the five years immediately preceding the calendar year in which the investment was made, paid a dividend on all the shares issued by it.

Thirdly, the Law Commission noted that trustees who needed more extensive powers than those conferred by the 1961 Act were required to go to the trouble and expense of applying to court in order that their powers could be extended. Indeed, the fact that such applications could successfully be made at all reflected the growing realisation that the provisions of the 1961 Act were inadequate. In the years following the coming into force of the 1961 Act, the courts were unprepared to accede to such applications except in special circumstances: it was held in *Re Kolb [1962] Ch 531* that the courts should regard the powers conferred by the 1961 Act as *prima facie* sufficient and should only be prepared to extend them in special cases. However, it was held in *Trustees of the British Museum v Attorney-General [1984] 1 WLR 418* that in view of changed conditions since the coming into force of the 1961 Act, in particular the high rates of inflation prevalent during much of the 1970s, and the corresponding changes in the investment market, the courts should again be prepared to entertain applications for increased powers of investment.

The distinction between narrower-range and wider-range investments and the requirement that the trust fund be divided into two parts were relatively quickly regarded as unsatisfactory. In 1982, a mere 21 years after the passing of the 1961 Act, the view was expressed in the Law Reform Committee's 23rd Report that the Act was 'tiresome, cumbrous and expensive in operation'. The report also stated that 'the present statutory powers are out of date and ought now to be revised'.

However, other provisions of the 1961 Act have proved more durable. In particular, the provisions requiring a trustee to have regard to the need for diversification of the trust's investments and to the suitability of types of investment and of particular investments are largely re-enacted in the Trustee Act 2000 as the 'standard investment criteria' set out in section 4 of that Act.

Powers of investment conferred on trustees by the Trustee Investments Act 1961

Power to invest in narrower-range investments

9.5   By section 1(1) of the Trustee Investments Act 1961, a trustee was permitted to invest any property in his hands, whether at the time in a state of investment or not, in any manner specified in Part I or II of Schedule 1 to the Act. This provision is subject to section 1(3), which sets out the circumstances in which the powers conferred by the Act will be excluded: see further the discussion at 9.12 below.

'Property' is defined in section 4(1) of the 1961 Act so as to include real or personal property of any description, including money and things in action; it does not include an interest in expectancy, although the falling into possession of such an interest or the receipt of the proceeds of sale thereof is treated as an accrual of property to the trust fund.

An investment falling within Part I or II of Schedule 1 to the Act was defined as a 'narrower-range investment' by section 1(4). The investments specified in Part I of Schedule 1 were those whose capital value is constant, such as Defence Bonds. Part II contained investments which broadly correspond to the 'statutory list' of investments which trustees had been permitted to make under the Trustee Act 1925. The distinction between the investments specified in Part I and those contained in Part II is that trustees were obliged to obtain and consider advice before making the second type of investment (see 9.24 below).

Power to invest in wider-range investments

9.6   By section 1(1) of the 1961 Act, a trustee was permitted to invest in any manner specified in Part III of Schedule 1 to the Act, subject to the provisions of section 2. An investment falling within Part III is defined as a 'wider-range investment' by section 1(4). The presence of the investments specified in Part III (which, significantly, included equities) ensured that the Act represented an important extension of trustees' investment powers over the previous law.

The restrictions on trustees' powers to invest in wider-range investments were contained in section 2. By section 2(1) a trustee did not have the power to make or retain any such investment unless the trust fund had been divided into two parts, referred to as the narrower-range part and the wider-range part. Where such a division had been made, no subsequent division of the same fund might be made for the purposes of section 2.

By virtue of section 2(2) of the Act, trustees were not permitted to invest property belonging to the narrower-range part of the trust fund except in narrower-range investments. By contrast, no restriction was imposed in relation to property belonging to the wider-range part of the fund; it could be invested in either wider-range or narrower-range investments, or in any combination of the two. Thus, the 1961 Act ensured that at least half of the value of the trust fund following division would be invested in narrower-range investments.

Alteration in the proportions into which the fund was to be divided

9.7 Originally, the two parts of the fund were to be equal in value at the time of the division. However, section 13(1) of the 1961 Act provided that the Treasury might direct, by order made by statutory instrument, that any division of a trust fund pursuant to section 2(1) should be made so that the value of the wider-range part would bear to the value of the narrower-range part such proportion as might be prescribed by the order, that proportion being greater than 1 but not greater than 3:1. A proportion of 3:1 was prescribed by the Trustee Investments (Division of Trust Fund) Order 1996 (SI 1996/845).

Notwithstanding that only one division of a trust fund was permitted under section 2(1), section 13(2) provided that a fund which had been divided before the coming into force of an order made under section 13(1) could be divided once again in the proportions specified in that order. By section 13(4) an order made pursuant to section 13(1) could be revoked by a subsequent order prescribing a greater proportion; however, since the 1996 Order prescribed the maximum permitted proportion of 3:1 and no power was conferred on the Treasury to provide that the specified proportion be reduced, no further order could in fact have been made.

Holding the balance between the two parts of the fund

9.8 It was further provided by section 2(2) of the 1961 Act that if property which was not invested in narrower-range investments became comprised in the narrower-range part of the fund, for example through property accruing to that part of the fund under section 2(3) (see 9.10 below), a trustee had to ensure that the balance between narrower- and wider-range investments was held in one of two ways.

First, the property which was not invested in narrower-range investments could be transferred to the wider-range part of the fund, in which case a 'compensating transfer', defined as 'a transfer in the opposite direction of property of equal value', was also required to be made. Secondly, it was provided that the trustee might reinvest the property concerned in narrower-range investments 'as soon as may be'.

Transfers from one part of a trust fund to the other

9.9 By virtue of section 2(1) of the 1961 Act, a trustee was not permitted to transfer property from the narrower-range part of the fund to the wider-range part (or vice versa) unless one of two conditions was satisfied:

- such a transfer was authorised or required by the provisions of the Act itself; or

- a compensating transfer was made at the same time.

Accrual of property to the trust fund

9.10   The position where property accrued to a trust fund after the fund had been divided was dealt with by section 2(3). If the property accrued to the trustee as owner or former owner of property comprised in either part of the fund, it was to be treated as belonging to that part of the fund (Trustee Investments Act 1961, s 2(3)(a)). Thus, for example, shares received by trustees under a bonus issue belonged to the wider-range part of the fund. Otherwise, the trustee was obliged to secure that the value of each part of the fund was increased by the same amount, either by apportionment of the accruing property or the transfer of property from one part of the fund to the other, or both.

Property taken out of the trust fund

9.11   It was provided by section 2(4) of the 1961 Act that where, in the exercise of any power or duty of a trustee, property fell to be taken out of the trust fund, the provisions of section 2 would not restrict his discretion as to the choice of property to be taken out. This subsection covered, for example, situations where the trustee was required to pay taxes due or proposed to exercise a power of advancement over capital. Its effect was that the trustee would have been permitted to raise the necessary funds entirely from the narrower-range part of the fund if he saw fit. In this way, the proportion of the fund belonging to the narrower-range part could be significantly reduced.

Exclusion of the powers conferred by the 1961 Act

9.12   The ability of settlors and testators to exclude the powers conferred on trustees by section 1 of the 1961 Act was dealt with by the provisions of section 1(3). This subsection drew a distinction between instruments made before the passing of the Act on 3 August 1961 and those made afterwards.

Instruments made before the passing of the 1961 Act

9.13   By virtue of section 1(3) of the 1961 Act, no provision relating to the powers of a trustee contained in any instrument made before the passing of the Act could limit the powers conferred by section 1. 'Instrument' in this context did not include an enactment or an instrument made under an enactment.

Instruments made after the passing of the 1961 Act

9.14   By contrast, section 1(3) provided that the powers conferred by the Act were exercisable only in so far as a contrary intention was not expressed in any instrument made after the passing of the Act (except one made under an enactment, which could exclude the powers conferred by the Act whenever made).The words 'in so far as a contrary intention is not expressed' also appeared in the same context in section 69(2) of the Trustee Act 1925. Simonds J held in *Re Warren [1939] Ch 684* that this provision fell to be construed in the same way as the words 'unless expressly forbidden' in section 1 of the Trustee Act 1893. Its effect was that a trust instrument would not restrict the statutory powers merely by conferring on trustees a more restrictive power of investment than the statutory power – an express provision that the trustees might not invest in any way other than those specified in the instrument was necessary. (See, for example, *Re Burke [1908] 2 Ch 248*: 'my trustees shall keep my trust estate and invest the same by leaving the same on deposit with the said bank at such rate of interest as they may be able to obtain' where it was held that the statutory power was not excluded; see also *Ovey v Ovey [1900] 2 Ch 524*: accumulations of income to be invested in 3% consolidated bank annuities 'and no other securities', where it was held that the statutory power was excluded.)

Relationship between powers conferred by the 1961 Act and other powers of investment

Special powers

9.15   Section 3(1) of the Act provided that the powers conferred by the Act were in addition to and not in derogation from any other powers of investment (or of postponing conversion) exercisable by a trustee. Such a power was defined as a 'special power'.

By virtue of section 3(2), a special power to invest property in any investment for the time being authorised by law for the investment of trust property took effect as a power to invest property in like manner and subject to the like provisions as under the foregoing provisions of the Act. This subsection therefore made clear that the provisions of the Act would apply to a trust which contained a power of investment in these terms.

Special-range property

9.16   Section 3(3), supplemented by Schedule 2 to the Act, introduced the additional concept of 'special-range property'. Special-range property could include wider-range but not narrower-range investments. The term covered property which a trustee was authorised to hold apart from, first, the provisions of the Act itself or Part I of the Trustee Act 1925, or second, a power to invest property in investments for the time being authorised by law. It also covered property which became part of a trust fund in consequence of the exercise by a trustee, as owner of special-range property, of any power conferred by section 10(3) or 10(4) of the Trustee Act 1925. Subsection (3) permitted trustees of a trust fund including securities of a company to concur in various types of scheme or arrangement in relation to the company. By subsection (4), trustees were permitted, *inter alia*, to exercise any right to subscribe for securities in a company which was offered to them. Section 10 of the 1925 Act was repealed by the Trustee Act 2000.

Trust property which the trustees were authorised to hold by a special power therefore constituted special-range property even if the trustees would, in any case, have been permitted to hold it as a wider-range investment (though not as a narrower-range investment).

Paragraph 2(1) of Schedule 2 to the Act provided that where a trust fund included special-range property, the requirement (contained in section 2(1)) that the fund be divided applied only to so much of it as did not consist of special-range property. Such property was to be 'carried to a different part of the fund'. Therefore, if a trust fund with an overall value of £100,000 contained special-range property worth £50,000, the trustees would be required to invest only £25,000 of the remaining £50,000 (and, following the Trustee Investments (Division of Trust Fund) Order 1996, only £12,500) in narrower-range investments. As noted above, this would have been so even if the trustees would in any case have been authorised to hold the special-range property as wider-range investments.

Property converted into special-range property

9.17   Paragraph 2(2) of Schedule 2 provided that property belonging to the narrower-range or wider-range part of a trust fund which was converted into special-range property was also to be carried to a separate part of the fund containing such property. The same applied to special-range property which accrued to a trust fund after the division of the fund pursuant to section 2(1) (or part of the fund if it had contained special-range property at the time of division).

Property ceasing to be special-range property

9.18   Paragraph 2(3) of Schedule 2 dealt with the converse situation where property which had been carried to a separate part of the fund was converted into property other than special-range property. Such property was to be transferred to the narrower- or wider-range part of the fund or was to be apportioned between them. The two parts of the fund were to be increased by the same amount and any transfer of property from one part to the other was to be made which was necessary to achieve this.

Powers conferred or varied after 3 August 1951

9.19   Certain exceptions to the rules about special-range property were created by section 3(4) of the Act. This subsection provided that section 3(3) did not apply where the powers of a trustee to invest (or to postpone conversion) had been conferred or varied in one of the following two ways:

- by an order of the court made within the period of ten years ending with the passing of the Act (in other words, after 3 August 1951). As explained at 9.4 above, in the years before the passing of the 1961 Act numerous applications had been successfully made by trustees seeking to have their powers of investment extended under section 57 of the Trustee Act 1925, the Variation of Trusts Act 1958 or the court's inherent jurisdiction; or

- by any enactment passed (or instrument having effect under an enactment made) within that period which related specifically to the trusts in question.

If, therefore, immediately before the passing of the Act, a trustee was able to invest half his fund in equities, not because the trust instrument permitted him to do so but because he had been authorised to do so by a court order made in the previous ten years, he would not be able to take advantage of the provisions relating to special-range property.

Instead, the position would be governed by Schedule 3 to the Act. Paragraph 1 provided that where property belonging to the narrower-range part of a trust fund:

(a)   was invested otherwise than in narrower-range investments; or

(b)   being so invested, was retained and not transferred or as soon as may be reinvested in narrower-range investments pursuant to section 2(2),

then, so long as that situation continued, the trustee was not permitted to make or retain any wider-range investment under section 1. Paragraph 2 of Schedule 3 provided that section 4 of the Trustee Act 1925, which relieved a trustee from liability for retaining an investment which had ceased to be authorised, would not apply where the trustee ceased to be so authorised by virtue of paragraph 1. Section 4 of the 1925 Act was repealed by the Trustee Act 2000.

Appropriation of part of a trust fund to form a separate fund

9.20   The position where property was taken out of a trust fund by way of appropriation so as to form a separate fund was dealt with by section 4(3) of the Act. Funds were treated as separate if they were held on trusts which were not identical in respect of the beneficiaries or their respective interests or the purposes of the trust or the powers of the trustee (Trustee Investments Act 1961, s 4(2)).

If the trust fund from which property was appropriated had previously been divided pursuant to section 2(1) (or under those provisions as modified by the special-range property provisions contained in Schedule 2), then if the separate fund was also to be so divided, its narrower-range and wider-range parts might be constituted so as:

(a)   to be equal (following the making of the Trustee Investments (Division of Trust Fund) Order 1996 (SI 1996/845) (as to which see 9.7 above) the applicable proportion would have been 3:1 rather than equality); or

(b)   to bear to each other the same proportion as the two corresponding parts of the original fund as at the time of appropriation; or

(c)   some intermediate proportion.

Thus, if (before 1996) a trust fund had been constituted so that, by virtue of greater appreciation of the wider-range part of the fund than the narrower-range part, 60% of the fund belonged to the former part at the time of an appropriation to a separate fund, the trustees would have been permitted to divide the separate fund equally, or in the ratio 60:40, or in some intermediate proportion. Given the greater flexibility offered by having as large a wider-range part as possible (since property belonging to that part could be invested in either narrower- or wider-range investments as the trustees saw fit), trustees making such a decision would invariably have selected the second option.

Valuations of the trust fund

9.21   In order to take advantage of the provisions of the 1961 Act by investing in wider-range investments, trustees were required to divide the trust fund into two parts of equal value as has been seen. Moreover, if an appropriation was afterwards made to a separate fund which the trustees also proposed to divide, a further valuation was necessary in order to ascertain the relative values of the narrower- and wider-range parts of the fund – see 9.20 above). It was therefore important that a mechanism be established which allowed trustees to protect themselves in acting on the basis of valuations. Such provision was made by section 5 of the Act.

By virtue of section 5(1) a trustee would be protected if he obtained a valuation of any property from a person reasonably believed by the trustee to be qualified to make it. The valuation had to be in writing. If these conditions were met, the valuation was conclusive in determining whether the valuation had been duly made. This provision applied whether the valuation was sought for the purpose of:

•   division of the fund under section 2(1); or

•   the making of a compensating transfer under section 2(1) or 2(2); or

•   carrying special-range property to a separate part of the fund under Schedule 2.

By virtue of section 5(2), section 5(1) applied to a valuation made by a person in the course of his employment as an officer or servant. Thus, a corporate trustee might obtain a valuation from one of its own employees whom it reasonably believed to be appropriately qualified.

Trustees' duties in choosing investments

9.22   Apart from restricting the extent to which trustees could invest in wider-range securities such as equities, the other way in which the 1961 Act sought to regulate trustees' powers of investment was by imposing duties relating to the way in which investments were chosen. These duties were contained in section 6 of the Act.

Diversification and suitability

9.23   Section 6(1) provided that in the exercise of his powers of investment a trustee was to have regard to two factors:

•   the need for diversification of investments of the trust, in so far as was appropriate to the circumstances of the trust;

•   the suitability to the trust of investments of the description of investment proposed and of the investment proposed as an investment of that description.

This provision applied to an exercise by a trustee of his powers of investment whether those powers were conferred by the trust instrument or by the Act itself; in the latter case it applied whether the proposed investments were in narrower-range or wider-range investments.

Investments which required trustees to obtain advice

9.24   Section 6(2) provided that before exercising his powers of investment in certain specified ways, a trustee was required to obtain and consider proper advice on the question whether the investment was satisfactory having regard to the matters mentioned in section 6(1)(a) and (b), namely the need for diversification and the suitability to the trust of the investment proposed. Advice was to be sought by a trustee before exercising any power conferred:

•   by section 1 of the Act, to invest in a manner specified in Part II or III of Schedule 1;

•   by section 3(2) of the Act (which concerns special powers to invest property 'in any investment for the time being authorised by law for the investment of trust property'), to invest in such a manner.

It was in relation to the taking of advice that a distinction was made between investments specified in Parts I and II of Schedule 1 to the Act. Although both parts contained narrower-range investments, a trustee was only required to take advice before investing in a manner set out in Part II. By contrast, advice was considered unnecessary in the context of those investments contained in Part I since their capital value could not fluctuate.

Retaining of an investment

9.25   Section 6(3) extended the requirement that the trustee obtain and consider proper advice to the situation where he retained an investment which had been made in the exercise of a power conferred by Part II or III or in the exercise of a power falling within section 3(2) (see 9.24 above). In that event he was required to determine at what intervals the circumstances, and in particular the nature of the investment, made it desirable for him to obtain advice, and then to obtain and consider it accordingly.

Advice to be obtained and considered

9.26   It should be noted that a trustee was required by the provisions of section 6 only to 'obtain and consider' proper advice; he was not required to act upon its recommendations since this would have removed his discretion. That said, a trustee who did not follow proper advice which he had received would inevitably potentially expose himself to allegations that he had not properly exercised his powers of investment.

Proper advice

9.27   Only in taking proper advice would a trustee comply with the requirements of section 6. This was defined in section 6(4) as 'the advice of a person who is reasonably believed by the trustee to be qualified by his ability in and practical experience of financial matters'. The subsection further provided that proper advice might be given by a person giving it in the course of his employment as an officer or servant. This provision mirrors that in relation to the obtaining of a valuation by a trustee contained in section 5(2) (see 9.21 above).

Advice to be given or confirmed in writing

9.28   In order to comply with section 6(2) and (3), the advice obtained and considered had to be given, or else subsequently confirmed, in writing (Trustee Investments Act 1961, s 6(5)).

Advice given by one of the trustees

9.29   Section 6(6) provided that the requirement that a trustee obtain and consider proper advice did not apply to one of two or more trustees where he was the person giving the advice required by the section to his co-trustee or co-trustees. If, therefore, one of the trustees of a fund was himself qualified to give advice on financial matters so as to satisfy the requirements of section 6(4) (as to which see 9.27 above) and the other trustee(s) took his advice, it was not necessary for him to seek advice himself.

The subsection also provided that the advice requirement did not apply where powers of a trustee were lawfully exercised by an officer or servant competent to give financial advice within the meaning of section 6(4). Accordingly, a corporate trustee was not required to take investment advice where its powers of investment were exercised by an officer or servant who was himself competent to give the advice in question.

Chapter 10

Breach of Trust

General principles

10.1   If a trustee commits a breach of trust, traditionally the trustee's liability is essentially to restore the trust property as it was before the breach. The trustee must either restore to the trust the actual trust property lost by reason of the breach or pay compensation for such loss. The introduction of the Trustee Act 2000 should not have altered this position. The new statutory duty of care is a duty imposed on trustees in their character as such and is intended to codify the duty that formerly arose under the general law. The correct cause of action should therefore remain breach of trust, rather than breach of statutory duty, which is a tortious cause of action giving rise to a claim in damages where appropriate.

Application of the principles

10.2   The principles applicable to claims for breach of trust were considered by the House of Lords in the case of *Target Holdings Ltd v Redferns [1996] AC 421*. This case was essentially a professional negligence case where a mortgage company was suing the solicitor who had acted for it on a mortgage transaction. In addition to making claims in contract and tort against the solicitor the claimant alleged breach of trust. Its case was that the solicitor misapplied the mortgage money paid to its client's account for the purpose of enabling the solicitors to complete the transaction. Because the property market had fallen, the claimant wished to claim the whole of the money paid away notwithstanding that if the transaction had successfully completed without breach, it would still have suffered a loss due to the fall in property values. It was not, therefore, a case involving a traditional trust where property is held for beneficiaries on a long-term basis. However, their Lordships restated principles that are applicable to such traditional trusts and it is worthwhile quoting extensively from this judgment as it provides guidance as to how a modern court approaches long-established principles. Some older cases may have to be viewed in the light of what was said in *Target*.

Lord Browne-Wilkinson said as follows:

> 'At common law there are two principles fundamental to the award of damages. First, that the defendant's wrongful act must cause the damage

complained of. Second, that the plaintiff is to be put "in the same position as he would have been in if he had not sustained the wrong for which he is now getting his compensation or reparation" (see *Livingstone v Rawyards Coal Co (1880) 5 App Cas 25 at 39* per Lord Blackburn). Although, as will appear, in many ways equity approaches liability for making good a breach of trust from a different starting point, in my judgement those two principles are applicable as much in equity as at common law. Under both systems liability is fault-based: the defendant is only liable for the consequences of the legal wrong he has done to the plaintiff and to make good the damage caused by such wrong. He is not responsible for damage not caused by his wrong or to pay by way of compensation more than the loss suffered from such wrong. The detailed rules of equity as to causation and the quantification of loss differ, at least ostensibly, from those applicable at common law. But the principles underlying both systems are the same'.

The remedy for a breach of trust is not damages at common law but rather equitable compensation. The *Target* case makes it clear that questions of causation are relevant and that the principles applicable to claims for breach of trust are fundamentally the same those that apply to common law claims in contract and tort.

As Lord Browne-Wilkinson went on to say:

'There can be cases where, although there is an undoubted breach of trust, the trustee is under no liability at all to a beneficiary. For example, if a trustee commits a breach of trust with the acquiescence of one beneficiary, that beneficiary has no right to complain and an action for breach of trust brought by him would fail completely. Again there may be cases where the breach gives rise to no right to compensation. Say, as often occurs, a trustee commits a judicious breach of trust by investing in an unauthorised investment which proves to be very profitable to the trust. A carping beneficiary could insist that the unauthorised investment be sold and the proceeds invested in authorised investments: but the trustee would be under no liability to pay compensation either to the trust fund or to the beneficiary because the breach has caused no loss to the trust fund. Therefore, in each case the first question is to ask what are the rights of the beneficiary: only if some relevant right has been infringed so as to give rise to a loss is it necessary to consider the extent of the trustee's liability to compensate for such loss.

The basic right of a beneficiary is to have the trust duly administered in accordance with the provisions of the trust instrument, if any, and the general law. Thus, in relation to a traditional trust where the fund is held in trust for a number of beneficiaries having different, usually successive, equitable interests, (eg A for life with remainder to B), the right of each beneficiary is to have the whole fund vested in the trustees so as to be available to satisfy his equitable interest when, and if, it falls into possession. Accordingly, in the case of a breach of such a trust involving the wrongful paying away of trust assets, the liability of the trustee is to restore to the trust fund, often called "the trust estate", what ought to have been there.

The equitable rules of compensation for breach of trust have been largely developed in relation to such traditional trusts, where the only way in which all the beneficiaries' rights can be protected is to restore to the trust fund what ought to be there. In such a case the basic rule is that a trustee in breach of trust must restore or pay to the trust estate either the assets which have been lost to the estate by reason of the breach or compensation for such loss. Courts of Equity did not award damages but, acting in personam, ordered the defaulting trustee to restore the trust estate (see *Nocton v Lord Ashburton [1914] AC 932 at 952, 958, [1914–15] All ER Rep 45 at 51, 55* per Viscount Haldane LC). If specific restitution of the trust property is not possible, then the liability of the trustee is to pay sufficient compensation to the trust estate to put it back to what it would have been had the breach not been committed (see *Caffrey v Darby (1801) 6 Ves 488, [1775–1802] All ER Rep 507* and *Clough v Bond (1838) 3 My & Cr 490, 40 ER 1016*). Even if the immediate cause of the loss is the dishonesty or failure of a third party, the trustee is liable to make good that loss to the trust estate if, but for the breach, such loss would not have occurred (see Underhill and Hayton *Law of Trusts and Trustees* (14th edn, 1987) pp 734–736, *Re Dawson (decd), Union Fidelity Trustee Co Ltd v Perpetual Trustee Co Ltd [1966] 2 NSWR 211* and *Bartlett v Barclays Bank Trust Co Ltd (Nos 1 and 2) [1980] 2 All ER 92, [1980] Ch 515*). Thus the common law rules of remoteness of damage and causation do not apply. However, there does have to be some causal connection between the breach of trust and the loss to the trust estate for which compensation is recoverable, viz the fact that the loss would not have occurred but for the breach (see also *Re Miller's Deed Trusts (1978) 75 LS Gaz 454* and *Nestle v National Westminster Bank plc [1994] 1 All ER 118, [1993] 1 WLR 1260*). . . .

. . . A trustee who wrongly pays away trust money, like a trustee who makes an unauthorised investment, commits a breach of trust and comes under an immediate duty to remedy such breach. If immediate proceedings are brought, the court will make an immediate order requiring restoration to the trust fund of the assets wrongly distributed or, in the case of an unauthorised investment, will order the sale of the unauthorised investment and the payment of compensation for any loss suffered. But the fact that there is an accrued cause of action as soon as the breach is committed does not in my judgment mean that the quantum of the compensation payable is ultimately fixed as at the date when the breach occurred. The quantum is fixed at the date of judgment, at which date, according to the circumstances then pertaining, the compensation is assessed at the figure then necessary to put the trust estate or the beneficiary back into the position it would have been in had there been no breach. I can see no justification for 'stopping the clock' immediately in some cases but not in others: to do so may, as in this case, lead to compensating the trust estate or the beneficiary for a loss which, on the facts known at trial, it has never suffered'.

In rejecting the stop the clock approach, Lord Browne-Wilkinson went on to state that the equitable compensation for breach of trust has to be assessed as at the date of judgment and not at an earlier date. Losses are to be assessed as at the time of trial, using the full benefit of hindsight. Equitable compensation for breach of trust is designed to achieve exactly what the word compensation suggests: to make good a loss in fact suffered by the beneficiaries and which, using hindsight and common sense, can be seen to have been caused by the breach.

Unauthorised investments

10.3   In a breach of trust case involving investment, the above principles are especially pertinent. If unauthorised investments have been made then there may be a breach of trust but the first question to ask is whether this has, in fact, caused loss. The investments in question might have done well or at least done as well as other authorised investments that could have been made at the same time. Rises and falls in the stock market may mean that authorised investments would have fared just as badly and common sense and hindsight may be valuable mitigating factors for a trustee who has committed a breach of trust. This is perhaps particularly so in the new era of the Trustee Act 2000. The Act imposes new duties on trustees to take appropriate advice, to have regard to the 'standard investment criteria' and to exercise the statutory duty of care when making and changing investments. There will undoubtedly be many cases where breaches of these duties occur but perfectly sound investments are made and no loss is suffered. In other cases there may be losses but the trustee may be able to establish on the evidence that a similar degree of loss would have been suffered if the trustee had complied in every detail with his statutory obligations.

The old cases concerning breach of trust in relation to investment need to be approached with a degree of caution in that a modern court is likely to apply and in some cases modify them to accord with the general principles outlined by the House of Lords in *Target*.

Failure to invest

10.4   As we have seen, trustees are under a duty to invest the trust fund (see 1.11). In the case of *Attorney-General v Alford (1855) 4 De GM & G 843*, a trustee who delayed in investing was held liable to pay interest during the period of delay together with costs. The fact that a trustee does not make personal use of the money in the period does not afford any defence even if the trustee keeps the trust fund in a separate bank account (*Franklin v Frith (1792) 3 Bro CC 433; Treves v Townshend (1783) 1 Bro CC 384; Re Hilliard (1790) 1 Ves 89*). In the same way, trustees who were directed to accumulate income, ie to reinvest it, and who failed to do so were held liable to pay compound interest (*Raphael v Boehm (1807) 13 Ves 407; Re Emmet's Estate (1881) 17 Ch D 142*). In a case where non-investment of a trust fund persists for some time, it is likely that a modern court would not limit the equitable compensation payable to interest. The old cases date from an era when trust funds were seldom invested in equities. It may be that nowadays a court would assess compensation on the basis of expert evidence as to what the fund, if properly invested in a typical average diversified portfolio, would have achieved. Thus in a case where trustees invest a large fund in a deposit account pending a decision by them as to how to invest the fund, and they delay for an unreasonable time in making or implementing a decision to invest, the court might well award compensation on the basis of what the fund value would have been if it had been invested at the proper time.

Failure to follow directions as to investment

10.5   In a case where trustees were expressly directed to invest in a specified stock and failed to do so and kept the money in their hands, the beneficiaries were held entitled to elect to charge the trustees with the money or with the amount of stock they could have obtained if they had bought it when they should have done (*Shepherd v Mouls (1845) 4 Hare 500 at 504; Robinson v Robinson (1851) 1 De GM & G 247 at 256*). Nowadays, a court would have no difficulty in assessing equitable compensation on the basis of the value that the specified stock would have if purchased at the right time. In *Robinson v Robinson*, the trustees had been directed by their testator to realise his investments and invest the proceeds in one or other of two forms of investment; but the trustees had delayed the realisation of the testator's investments. When they actually sold they realised more than they would have realised if they had sold immediately after the testator's death, but less than if they had sold immediately after the testator's death and had thereupon invested the proceeds in one, rather than the other, of the two authorised forms of investment. It was sought to charge the trustees for what they would have received if they had followed that course of realisation and investment which in the event would have been the most favourable to the beneficiaries, but the court rejected that claim. The ratio, in the leading judgment of Lord Cranworth LJ, seems to have been in part that (*1 De GM & G 247 at 257–258, 42 ER 547 at 551*):

> 'Where a man is bound by covenants to do one of two things, and does neither, there in an action by the covenantee, the measure of damage is in general the loss arising by reason of the covenantor having failed to do that which is least, not that which is most, beneficial to the covenantee: and the same principle may be applied by analogy to the case of a trustee failing to invest in either of two modes equally lawful by the terms of the trust',

and in part that the liability of the trustee should not depend on the accident of the subsequent rise of one particular investment (see *1 De GM & G 247 at 259, 42 ER 547 at 552*). This case was, however, doubted in the modern case of *Nestle v National Westminster Bank plc [1994] 1 All ER 118* where Dillon LJ rejected the analogy drawn between a covenantee acting in his own interests who can choose the cheapest way to perform himself or get out of his obligations (*Lavarack v Woods of Colchester Ltd [1966] 3 All ER 683 at 690, [1967] 1 QB 278 at 293*) and a trustee who owes duties to his beneficiaries and cannot prefer his personal interest to theirs. The judge suggested instead that the appropriate course would have been to require the trustee to make good to the trust fair compensation – and not just the minimum that might just have got by without challenge – for failure to follow a proper investment policy.

Failure to invest in a prudent manner

10.6   *Nestle v National Westminster Bank plc [1994] 1 All ER 118, [1993] 1 WLR 1260* is a very important case in this area and one that is deserving of careful study. There, a testator died in 1922 leaving an estate worth £54,000. The defendant bank was appointed as trustee of the will. His widow was given a life interest in the family home and an annuity of £1,500. Subject to her interest, the estate was given to his two sons for life with remainders to their children. The widow died in 1960. In 1986 the plaintiff became solely entitled to the whole of the trust fund on the death of her father who was one of the testator's sons. The other son had died childless. The fund at that date was worth £269,000. The claimant brought a claim against the bank for breach of trust alleging that the fund should have been worth in excess of £1 million if the bank had discharged its investment duties with proper care. She alleged that:

- they failed to diversify investments and invest in equities between 1922 and 1960;

- failed to carry out regular reviews of the fund before 1959; and

- favoured the income beneficiaries over the capital beneficiaries at the expense of the plaintiff.

It was common ground that the bank had misconstrued its investment power. The relevant investment clause gave the trustee power to invest in:

'any securities or investments of the same or a similar nature to any belonging to the testator at the time of his death or in the stock, shares, bonds, debentures or securities of any railway or other company'.

The bank, without taking legal advice, regarded that clause as limiting its power to invest the trust funds in ordinary shares. It thought it could only invest in ordinary shares in companies in which the testator at death had a holding or in similar companies. After the Trustee Investments Act 1961 came into force it regarded its powers as wholly governed by that Act. In fact, the clause gave it power to invest in the stocks and shares of any company. The plaintiff's case on quantum was based on a comparison between the performance of the equities in the fund and the performance of the index of leading equity shares. Hoffmann J held that though the bank misconstrued its powers and acted in breach of trust the plaintiff had not proved that the breach had caused her any loss. The plaintiff appealed.

The Court of Appeal upheld the decision holding that although the bank had clearly failed in its duty to appreciate the scope of its powers of investment and had not reviewed the investments regularly, that was not sufficient to afford the plaintiff a remedy. The plaintiff had further to prove that the bank's failure to diversify the equities between 1922 and 1960 had caused her loss. It was not sufficient for her merely to prove loss of a chance that she would have been better off if the equities had been diversified, since it was necessary for her to prove that the annuity fund would have been worth more if a substantial proportion had been invested in equities rather than fixed interest securities or that the fund would have performed better if the bank had diversified out of the bank and insurance shares. In the absence of such proof, no loss had been proved. Although the bank had not been an effective manager of the trust investments under its control, it had not been shown to have committed any breach of trust resulting in loss.

A comparison with the composition of the equity shares index was insufficient to prove any loss because that index was calculated by reference to the perform-ance of leading equity shares and the composition of the list changed with companies' fortunes and therefore could not be the criterion for the degree of performance expected of the ordinary prudent trustee. There being no other evidence of loss, the claim in respect of the bank investment policy as trustee between 1922 and 1960 failed. The claim therefore failed for forensic reasons in that the method by which the plaintiff's legal team sought to prove her loss was rejected as inappropriate.

Evidence of loss

10.7   Although the particular claim failed, it is clear that it might have succeeded if proper evidence proving loss had been produced. The Court of Appeal rejected the use of the BZW equity index because it was an index that was difficult to beat, particularly for a fund which is not large enough to include substantial holdings in all the leading equities. It could not be the criterion for the degree of performance expected of the ordinary prudent trustee. Dillon LJ said that what the prudent man should do at any time depends on the economic and financial conditions pertaining at the particular time and not on what judges of the past have held to be the prudent course in the conditions of 50 or 100 years before.

Staughton LJ commented that life assurance companies and pension funds were not a reliable guide as to what would have been done by private investors or what should have been done by trustees of a private family trust. This was because such pension fund trustees and life companies were bound to follow a policy with considerable caution in order to ensure that, come what may, their minimum obligation in monetary terms was fulfilled.

Proper measure of damages

10.8   The best guidance on what the proper measure of damages should be in a *Nestle* type case was provided by Staughton LJ, who rejected the proposi-tion that compensation should be measured by the difference between the actual performance of the fund and the very least that a prudent trustee might have achieved. Instead, he preferred a comparison with what a prudent trustee was likely to have achieved – in other words, the average performance of ordinary shares during the period.

In the New Zealand case of *Re Mulligan [1998] 1 NZLR 481*, the claimants succeeded in proving breach of trust and also the loss suffered. A testator died in 1949 leaving his widow a substantial legacy and a life interest in a farm with nephews and nieces as residual beneficiaries. The trustees of the estate were a trustee company and the widow. The farm was sold in 1965 and the estate invested in fixed-interest securities until the widow died in 1990. Between 1965 and 1990 different trust company officers tried to persuade the widow to invest in shares to counter inflation but she adamantly refused to agree or allow direct contact with beneficiaries by the trust company. The widow bought a rental property in 1965, her own home with a rental flat in 1972 and (unknown to the trust company) owned a significant value of shares. At the widow's death, the capital of the testator's estate was in real terms a small proportion of what it was in 1965. The residual beneficiaries sued the trust company and widow for breach of trust on the basis that investing in fixed interest securities rather than shares did not treat the income and capital beneficiaries even-handedly. The trustees denied breach and relied on section 73 of the Trustee Act 1956 which provided that a trustee acting honestly and reasonably could be excused for breach of trust and failing to obtain directions of the court. The trustees also sought indemnities from each other.

Pankhurst J held that the discharge of a trustee's duty to act with due diligence and prudence was flexible and changed with economic conditions and contemporary thinking and was, therefore, judged applying the standards of the relevant period. A trustee had to be strictly impartial and even-handed between income and capital beneficiaries in the circumstances of the case. The trustees were in breach of trust because the trust company officers all recognised the corrosive harm of inflation to the estate capital (which was reliable evidence of the standard of prudence in the industry at the time) and should have attempted to persuade the widow by explaining the trustees' duty to be even-handed or applied to the court for directions rather than deferring to her wishes, particularly given her self-evident conflict of interest and preoccupation with maximising income from the estate.

The statutory defence in section 73 of the Act did not apply because:

(*a*)   the trust company did nothing adequate to persuade the widow to invest in shares and did not seek the court's directions; and

(*b*)   the widow did not act reasonably as a trustee as she was alive to the wisdom of shares by her own investments yet hostile to diversification by the estate and blocked contact by the trust company with residuary beneficiaries.

The court went on to hold that a defaulting trustee's obligation was to effect restitution to the trust. The measure of damages was therefore the value of trust assets at the date of restoration which a prudent trustee would have achieved using the best form of available investment. It was agreed that shares were the best available investment. The trustees should have invested in shares in 1972 (given the widow's substantial income from the trust since 1965, rents and share portfolio) at a prudent level of 40% of the estate (allowing a reasonable spread of shares and given inflation of about 10%). The plaintiffs would therefore have judgment for 40% of the capital in 1972 multiplied by the increase in the New Zealand shares index less a discount for lower risk investment, weighting of the index to successful shares and commissions on share dealings.

Investment in shares a matter of impression

10.9   The *Nestle* decision was relied on by both sides in the *Mulligan* case. This was not surprising as it remains one of the few reported decisions dealing with breach of trust of this type. The plaintiffs in *Mulligan* did not make the error made by Miss Nestle. They came armed with five expert witnesses. Pankhurst J commented that cases of this kind depend on their individual facts. The case was much more stark than that of *Nestle*. Because there had been no investment in equities for capital growth, it was much easier to prove the damage suffered. In considering the measure of damages, Pankhurst J adopted the approach that Staughton LJ said he would have adopted if he had got that far, that is to compare the actual fund performance with what a prudent trustee should have achieved, ie an average performance based on ordinary shares. Pankhurst J said the issue of when and to what extent the trustees should have invested in shares must be a matter of impression and it was not susceptible of detailed discussion. Applying this impressionistic approach, he held that by 1972 prudent trustees would have diversified to the extent of 40% of the then capital of the fund and invested that proportion in equities. The judge accepted evidence that while Barclays' index was a suitable benchmark it needed to be discounted to reflect the fact that an estate could not hope to buy the index which was a measure of successful shares. Shares in profitable companies entered the index and those in unsuccessful companies dropped out of it. For an estate to match the index, a very high volume of trading would be necessary. The judge applied a discount of 25% which was less than the 50% contended for by the defendants' expert witness.

There will be cases, therefore, where trustees choose not to invest in equities for valid reasons and where this cannot be criticised. In a recent personal injury case, *Wells v Wells [1998] 3 All ER 481*, where the House of Lords provided guidance on how damages for personal injury should be assessed, Lord Lloyd said that the search for a prudent investment will always depend on the circumstances of the particular investor. For a plaintiff who is not in a position to take risk and who wishes to protect himself against inflation in the short term of up to ten years, it is clearly prudent to invest in index-linked Government stocks. It could not be assumed that he would invest in equities. Logically, the same applied to a plaintiff investing for the long term. There will be cases, therefore, where trustees choose not to invest in equities for valid reasons. In cases which involve trusts that benefit persons who are vulnerable, a conservative approach will be hard to attack.

Investments wrongly disposed of

10.10   If a trustee, in breach of trust, wrongfully sells investments or distributes them, then his obligation is to restore the investments to the trust fund. This applies in a case where trust investments are sold to enable the proceeds to be reinvested in unauthorised securities even where those securities have not depreciated (*Re Massingberd's Settlement (1890) 63 LT 296*). The beneficiaries have a choice: they can elect instead to take the value of the original investments at the date of judgment. If the investments wrongfully sold would have been sold anyway, then a beneficiary will be limited to the value of the investments at the date when they would have been sold rather than the value at the date of judgment (*Re Bell's Indenture [1980] 1 WLR 1217; Re Montagu's Settlement Trusts* (21 December 1983, unreported). Trustees bear the obligation of proving that the investments would have been sold and this will often be a matter of some difficulty. Beneficiaries, if they prefer, can opt to have the proceeds of sale of the investments wrongly sold plus interest. This is so, even where the investments would have depreciated if they had been retained (*Shepherd v Mouls (1854) 4 Hare 500 at 504; Watts v Girdlestone (1843) 6 Beav 188*).

Wrongful investments

10.11   If trustees invest in unauthorised investments then the beneficiaries can treat them as having failed to invest at all. If lawful investments have been sold then the trustees must restore these investments to the fund. However, the beneficiaries can elect instead to take the value of the original investments at trial or their value at date of sale plus interest. If the wrongful investment is made at the inception of the trust administration, then the beneficiaries are entitled to the value of the fund invested plus interest. The trustees, if they face one of the above money claims, are entitled to keep the unauthorised securities in order to reduce their loss (*Knott v Cottee (1852) 16 Beav 77*). It is open to beneficiaries to adopt the wrongful investments as part of the trust fund. However, in order to do this, all the beneficiaries must be of full age and full capacity and must agree to this.

The question arises whether a trustee who makes an investment but fails to comply with his duties under sections 4 and 5 of the Trustee Act 2000 (ie having regard to the standard investment criteria and taking advice) makes an unauthorised investment or not. It is thought that it is probably the case that failure to comply with the safeguards means that an investment made in purported exercise of the wide section 3 power or an express power would be unauthorised. In many cases this might not cause any loss. However, in a case where an investment, that might have been a perfectly reasonable choice if the safeguards had been complied with, performs badly, beneficiaries could, it seems, exercise their traditional remedies. This would mean the trustees having to restore to the fund the original value invested plus interest. Trustees could, therefore, find themselves liable for a fall in the market by virtue of their having failed to follow correct procedures. The dangers for a trustee are obvious. It is unclear whether a court would entertain an argument that the same investment would have been made if the trustees had complied with their duties under sections 4 and 5 and therefore they should not be made liable for a loss that is essentially due to a fall in the market.

Tax and breach of trust

10.12 Compensation for breach of trust is not liable to be reduced on the grounds that if the breach had not occurred, the fund would have suffered various tax charges (*Re Bell's Indenture [1980] 1 WLR 1217* and *Bartlett v Barclays Trust Co Ltd [1980] Ch 515*). A different approach was taken in the breach of fiduciary duty case of *O'Sullivan v Management Agency and Music Ltd [1985] QB 428* where the Court of Appeal considered that income tax should be deducted in assessing the terms on which various agreements should be set aside between a pop star and the agency that managed his affairs. In another breach of fiduciary duty case, *John v James [1986] STC 352*, Nicholls J declined to follow *O'Sullivan* on this issue. The approach taken in *Re Bell's Indenture* is, therefore, still probably the correct approach and both Underhill & Hayton and Lewin take this view. This approach is, however, perhaps somewhat out of line with what Lord Browne-Wilkinson said in *Target Holdings Ltd v Redferns* (see 10.2 above) where he said that compensation should be assessed in the light of common sense and with the full benefit of hindsight.

Trustee exemption clauses

10.13 A trustee facing a claim in breach of trust should always scrutinise the trust instrument to see if there is a trustee exemption clause. There have been a series of important recent cases on trustees' exemption clauses.

In *Armitage v Nurse [1997] 3 WLR 1046* the court had to construe a clause which stated:

> 'No Trustee shall be liable for any loss or damage which may happen to [P's] fund or any part thereof or the income thereof at any time from any cause whatsoever unless such loss or damage shall be caused by his own actual fraud'.

Millett LJ held that actual fraud meant what it said, ie it did not include equitable fraud but required actual dishonesty. He rejected an argument that a clause which purported to exclude all liability except for actual fraud was void either for repugnancy or as contrary to public policy. He held that since it was open to contracting parties to exclude liability for ordinary or even gross negligence, such an exclusion was also open to the parties to a settlement.

In *Bogg v Raper* (*1998*) *1 ITELR 267* the Court of Appeal had to consider a clause in the following terms:

> 'in the professed execution of the trusts and powers hereof, no trustee (other than a trust corporation) shall be liable for any loss to the trust premises arising by reason of any improper investment made in good faith or for the negligence or fraud of any agent employed by him or by any other trustee hereof although the employment of such agent was not strictly necessary or expedient, or by reason of any mistake or omission made in good faith by any trustee hereof or by reason of any other matter or thing except wilful or individual fraud or wrongdoing on the part of the trustee who is sought to be made liable.'

The acts alleged against the defendants were acts of negligence and not dishonesty. The question whether the clause covered the acts arose. The approach to construction of such clauses was argued in the case. It was common ground that such clauses should be restrictively construed and that anything that was not clearly within it should be treated as falling outside it. *Armitage v Nurse* was cited as authority for this proposition. However, counsel for the plaintiffs went further and argued that the contractual exclusion clause approach found in various cases, eg *The Emmanuel C [1983] 1 All ER 686*, should be employed. The principles were:

- since it is inherently improbable that one party to a contract should intend to absolve the other party from the consequences of the latter's own negligence, the court will presume a clause not to have that effect unless the contrary is plainly shown; and

- where words used are wide enough to cover negligent as well as non-negligent acts or omissions, but practically speaking the clause lacks substance if it is not construed as covering negligent acts or omissions, the court may in the circumstances of a given case infer that the parties intended to cover negligence but it need not do so.

Two related principles are in play:

- a party seeking to rely on an exemption clause bears the burden of proving that it applies to the facts. Any doubt will be resolved against him; and

- in situations of ambiguity the words of a document will be construed more strongly against the maker of the document who now seeks to rely on the words.

Millett LJ stated that in a contract these principles march together but that in a will or a settlement the principles pointed in different directions. The document is the unilateral work of the settlor/testator. There is no inherent improbability that he should intend to absolve his executors or trustees from liability for the consequences of their negligence. As a result, he held the executors/trustees accept office on the terms of a document for which they are not responsible and are entitled to have the document 'fairly construed according to the natural meaning of the words used'. He went on to hold that all the allegations were covered by the scope of the clause. In doing so, he construed the words 'wilful or individual fraud or wrongdoing' as meaning wilful and individual. He also had regard to the form of the precedent on which the clause in the case was based. This supported his view that the 'or' was to be read as 'and' (citing *Re Follett [1955] 2 All ER 22* – a case where some words were omitted by mistake and the court was prepared to supply omitted words on the basis of evidence of the precedent used).

Millett LJ also rejected the argument that the draftsman of a will could not rely on an exemption clause if he was appointed as executor.

Inconsistent clauses

10.14   Finally, in *Wight v Olswang [1998] NPC 111*, Ferris J had to consider two inconsistent clauses in a settlement. Clause 11 was an exclusion clause in wide terms. Clause 18 was an exclusion clause which seemed to cover much of the same ground but only applied to non-professional trustees (ie those not charging remuneration). The plaintiffs argued that clause 11 did not exempt paid trustees because, if it did, it would be repugnant to clause 18. In support they cited a contractual case, *Elderslie Steamship v Borthwick [1905] AC 93 HL*.

Two of their Lordships held that two inconsistent clauses rendered the document ambiguous with the result that the liability could not be said to have been excluded by plain words. Lord Halsbury, however, reached the same result by a different route holding that the narrower clause had to be construed as an exception to the wider clause.

Ferris J in *Wight v Olswang* held that the inconsistency between the two clauses was too great to be ignored and rejected the submission that the rule in *Elderslie* was not applicable to a non-contractual document. He held that it was applicable and that clause 11 could not apply to exempt paid trustees.

The area of trustee exemption clauses is currently under review by the Law Commission and it is expected that the protections afforded by such clauses will be curtailed by a new statute. As the law still stands, such clauses provide valuable protection.

Limitation

10.15   A claim for a negligent breach of trust falls under section 21(3) of the Limitation Act 1980. This imposes a six-year period which generally runs from the date of breach and not from the date of damage (see *Re Somerset [1894] 1 Ch 231*). Section 14A of the Limitation Act 1980 applies to claims in tort and so will not extend the period for a breach of trust claim.

However, section 21(1) of the 1980 Act provides that no period of limitation shall apply to an action by a beneficiary under a trust being an action:

(*a*)   in respect of any fraud or fraudulent breach of trust to which the trustee was party or privy; or

(*b*)   to recover from the trustee trust property or the proceeds of trust property in the possession of the trustee, or previously received by the trustee.

A claim for breach of trust relating to investment will seldom involve fraud or conversion of trust property by the trustee, and so a six-year period running from the date of the breach will often be applicable.

However, section 21(3) provides that in the case of a beneficiary with a future interest the right of action shall not be treated as having accrued to any beneficiary until the interest fell into possession. Therefore, any beneficiary with a contingent or reversionary interest will not be barred. Further and more importantly, it has been held that a beneficiary under a discretionary trust has a future interest for the purpose of section 21(3) (*Armitage v Nurse [1998] Ch 241 at 261*).

Section 32 of the Limitation Act 1980 will prevent time from running in cases of fraud or deliberate concealment. This requires an intentional concealment of the facts relevant to the plaintiff's right of action. Section 32 is capable of applying in cases where trustees are aware of their breach at the time when they commit it or become aware of it later but chose to conceal it.

Chapter 11

Pensions

Pension trustees' duty of investment

11.1   In *Cowan v Scargill [1985] Ch 270 at 292*, Sir Robert Megarry V-C held that 'the trusts of pension funds are in general governed by the ordinary law of trusts, subject to any contrary provision in the rules or other provisions which govern the trust'. Trustees of pension funds, like trustees of simple family trusts, are obliged at all times to exercise their powers in the interests of the whole class of beneficiaries. Indeed, in considering submissions made by Mr Arthur Scargill to the effect that the normal principles of investment might not apply to pension trusts, Megarry V-C suggested that the characteristics which separate such trusts from those by reference to which the principles in question were originally developed make it all the more important that trustees adhere to those principles:

> 'The large size of pension funds emphasises the need for diversification, rather than lessening it, and the fact that much of the fund has been contributed by members of the scheme seems to me to make it even more important that the trustees should exercise their powers in the best interests of the beneficiaries'.

That said, the courts have in the past accepted that pension trustees may need wider powers of investment than family trustees. In *Mason v Farbrother [1983] 2 All ER 1078* the trustees of the Co-operative Wholesale Society's Employees' Pension and Death Benefit Scheme, which had been established in 1929, sought *inter alia* an order under section 57 of the Trustee Act 1925 conferring upon them investment powers over and above those conferred on them by the trust deed and the Trustee Investments Act 1961. In *Re Kolb's Will Trusts [1962] Ch 531* it had been held that, following the passing of the 1961 Act, the courts should not accede to applications seeking further extensions to trustees' investment powers in the absence of special circumstances. In *Mason*, however, Judge Blackett-Ord V-C held that the fact that the trust fund in question was a pension fund 'with perhaps something of a public element in it', constituted such a special circumstance. These remarks were approved by Megarry V-C in *Trustees of the British Museum v Attorney-General [1984] 1 All ER 337*.

Power of investment of pension trustees

11.2   Section 34(1) of the Pensions Act 1995 confers on the trustees of a 'trust scheme' (ie 'an occupational pension scheme established under a trust' – Pensions Act 1995, s 124(1)) 'the same power to make an investment of any kind as if they were absolutely entitled to the assets of the scheme'. Since this power is in the same terms as that conferred on non-pension trustees by section 3(1) of the Trustee Act 2000, section 36(3) of that Act provides that Part II – the Part under which the general power of investment is conferred – does not apply to the trustees of an occupational pension scheme; neither does Part III, which deals with the acquisition of land. Moreover, the power conferred under the 1995 Act, like that under the Trustee Act 2000, is expressed by section 34(1) of the 1995 Act to be 'subject to any restriction imposed by the scheme'. That said, it seems improbable that it would be desired to give trustees of a pension scheme less flexibility in making investments than they would have under the 1995 Act.

Indeed, trust deeds establishing pension funds often give trustees wider powers of investment than they would otherwise have. Since the term 'investment' is not defined in the 1995 Act, it is possible that the purchase by trustees of a non-income producing asset would be open to criticism: see the discussion in CHAPTER 1 at paragraphs 1.5 to 1.6. (The Pension Law Review Committee regarded the term 'investment' as meaning 'any application of assets, whether or not investments in the technical sense' (Report of the Pension Law Review Committee, p 342).) Accordingly, it is generally desirable to include provisions specifically authorising trustees to engage in such purchases and other activities which arguably do not constitute investment in law, such as the purchase of traded options. Alternatively, trustees can be given power to invest *or otherwise apply* the assets of the fund as though they were absolute owners.

Duty of care

11.3   The duty of care imposed on trustees by Part I of the Trustee Act 2000 does not apply to the trustees of occupational pension schemes (Trustee Act 2000, s 36(2)). The duty which arises under the general law therefore continues to apply to pension trustees. The Pension Law Review Committee suggested that this duty should be incorporated into the Pensions Act 1995 but this recommendation was not followed by the Government, despite having been included in the White Paper.

Under the general law a trustee is required 'to take such care as an ordinary prudent man would take if he were minded to make an investment for the benefit of other people for whom he felt morally bound to provide'. However, where a trustee holds himself out as having some special skill over and above that of the ordinary prudent man of business the duty imposed on him will be correspondingly higher (*Bartlett v Barclays Bank Trust Co Ltd [1980] 2 WLR 430, 443–444*).

Exclusions

11.4   Section 33(1) of the Pensions Act 1995 prevents the exclusion or restriction by any instrument or agreement of liability for breach of an obligation under any rule of law to take care or exercise skill in the performance of any investment function. This prohibition applies whether the person in breach of duty is a trustee or a person to whom the investment function has been delegated under section 34 of the Act. By section 33(2), references to excluding or restricting liability include making the liability or its enforcement subject to restrictive or onerous conditions; excluding or restricting any right or remedy in respect of the liability, or subjecting a person to any prejudice in consequence of his pursuing any such right or remedy; or excluding or restricting rules of evidence or procedure. There is, however, no provision prohibiting indemnity clauses under which trustees in breach of their obligations are entitled to be indemnified out of the trust fund.

Written statement of investment principles

11.5   By virtue of section 35(1) of the Pensions Act 1995, pension trustees are obliged to secure that a written statement of the principles governing investment decisions for the purposes of the scheme is prepared, maintained and from time to time revised.

Trustees' policies

11.6   The matters to be dealt with in the statement are the trustees' policies in relation to the following (section 35(2) and (3)):

- securing compliance with section 36 of the Act, which deals with the need for diversification of investments, the suitability to the scheme of investments and the taking of advice as to whether an investment is satisfactory;

- securing compliance with section 56, which deals with the requirement (referred to in the 1995 Act as the 'minimum funding requirement') that the value of the assets of a scheme is not less than the amount of its liabilities;

- the kind of investments to be held;

- the balance between different kinds of investments;

- risk;

- the expected return on investments;

- the realisation of investments;

- such other matters as may be prescribed.

Regulation 11A of the Occupational Pension Schemes (Investment) Regulations 1996 (SI 1996/3127) (as amended by the Occupational Pension Schemes (Investment, and Assignment, Forfeiture, Bankruptcy etc) Amendment Regulations 1999 (SI 1999/1849)), provides that the trustees are to state their policy in relation to two matters:

- first, the extent (if at all) to which social, environmental or ethical considerations are taken into account in the selection, retention and realisation of investments;

- secondly, their policy (if any) in relation to the exercise of the rights (including voting rights) attaching to investments.

Obtaining written advice and the duty to consult the employer

11.7   By section 35(5) the trustees are obliged to do two things before a statement is prepared or revised:

- obtain and consider the written advice of a person whom they reasonably believe to be qualified by his ability in, and practical experience of, financial matters and to have the appropriate knowledge and experience of the management of the investments of occupational pension trust schemes;

- consult the employer, which means the employer of persons in the description or category of employment to which the scheme relates (Pensions Act 1995, s 124(1)). Where there is more than one employer, the trustees' duty is to consult the person who has been nominated by all the employers to act as their representative for the purposes of section 35(1)(b), if any; and if no person has been so nominated the trustees are required to consult all the employers (SI 1996/3127, reg 11(1)). In those circumstances, if the trustees specify a reasonable period of at least 28 days within which they must receive representations from the employers, they are not required to consider any representations received after that period (SI 1996/3127, reg 11(2)).

While the employer is to be consulted, however, section 35(4) prohibits restrictions on any power to make investments by reference to the consent of the employer from being imposed by either the trust instrument or the statement.

If a statement has not been prepared or is not being maintained, or the trustees have not obtained and considered advice in accordance with section 35(5)(a), any trustee who has failed to take all such steps as are reasonable to secure compliance with those requirements may be the subject of either a prohibition order under section 3 of the Act (under this section the Occupational Pensions Regulatory Authority (OPRA) may prohibit a person from being a trustee of a particular trust scheme in various prescribed circumstances) or a civil penalty under section 10 (by virtue of section 10, OPRA may require a person to pay a penalty).

Delegation

11.8   Before the passing of the Pensions Act 1995, trustees of pension funds were in the same position as other trustees as far as delegation was concerned. By section 23 of the Trustee Act 1925 they were entitled to employ and pay an agent to transact any business or do any act required to be transacted or done in the execution of the trust. However, this provision did not enable them to delegate the making of investment decisions since this would involve the agent in more than merely doing an act required in the execution of the trust.

Section 23 of the Trustee Act 1925 has now been repealed by section 11 of the Trustee Act 2000 which permits trustees to delegate any of their functions (with certain exceptions). See the discussion in CHAPTER 7: COLLECTIVE DELEGA- TION.

Although the relevant part of the Trustee Act 2000, Part IV, applies in general to trustees of a pension scheme, section 36(5) of that Act provides that such trustees may not authorise any person to exercise any functions relating to investment as their agent.

The reason for this exclusion is that provision for such delegation had already been made by section 34 of the Pensions Act 1995. By section 34(2), any discretion of pension trustees to make investment decisions may, subject to any restriction imposed by the scheme, be delegated to a fund manager who can take the decisions in question without contravening section 19 of the Financial Services and Markets Act 2000.

Provided the trustees (or the person who made the delegation on their behalf) have taken all reasonable steps to satisfy themselves:

*   that the fund manager has the appropriate knowledge and experience for managing the investments of the scheme; and

*   that he is carrying out his work competently and is complying with section 36 of the Act,

they are not responsible for any act or default of the fund manager (Pensions Act 1995, s 34(4)).

Further powers of delegation

11.9   By section 34(5) pension trustees are given two further powers of delegation. Again subject to any restriction imposed by the scheme, they may:

*   authorise two or more of their number to exercise on their behalf any discretion to make any decision about investments;

*   delegate any such discretion to a fund manager who is neither authorised nor exempt within the meaning of section 19 of the Financial Services and

Markets Act 2000 where giving effect to the decision made would not constitute the carrying on of a regulated activity within the meaning of that Act.

By contrast with the power of delegation under section 34(2), the trustees will remain liable in either case for any acts or defaults in the exercise of the discretion. However, section 33 of the Act, which prevents the exclusion of liability for breach of an obligation to take care or exercise skill in the performance of an investment function, does not prevent the exclusion or restriction of any liability of the trustees for the acts or defaults of a fund manager in exercising a discretion delegated to him under section 34(5)(b) provided the trustees have taken all reasonable steps to satisfy themselves of the matters set out at 11.8 above (section 34(6)).

Choosing investments

11.10 Section 36(2) of the Pensions Act 1995 provides that the trustees of a pension scheme in exercising their powers of investment, or a fund manager to whom a discretion has been delegated under section 34 of the Act in exercising that discretion, must have regard to two matters:

- the need for diversification of investments, in so far as appropriate to the circumstances of the scheme;

- the suitability to the scheme of investments of the description of investment proposed and of the investment proposed as an investment of that description.

By section 36(3) the trustees, before investing in any manner except those set out in Part I of the First Schedule to the Trustee Investments Act 1961 ('narrower-range investments not requiring advice'), must obtain and consider proper advice on the question whether the investment is satisfactory having regard both to the section 36(2) factors and the principles contained in the statement which the trustees are obliged to have prepared under section 35. Where the giving of such advice constitutes a regulated activity under the Financial Services and Markets Act 2000, proper advice will be that given by a person who may give it without contravening the prohibition imposed by section 19 of that Act; otherwise, the meaning of 'proper advice' will be the same as for the purposes of section 35(5) – see 11.7 above. The advice taken must be given or subsequently confirmed in writing (Pensions Act 1995, s 36(7)).

As well as taking proper advice before undertaking investment, trustees *retaining* an investment must determine at what intervals the circumstances and the nature of the investment make it desirable to obtain such advice and act accordingly (Pensions Act 1995, s 36(4)).

The provisions of section 36 of the 1995 Act largely reproduce section 6 of the Trustee Investments Act 1961 (this section was repealed by the Trustee Act

2000). Indeed, certain of the provisions of the earlier Act, such as the requirement to diversify, broadly state trustees' obligations at common law. However,
section 36 of the 1995 Act also includes provisions peculiar to pension trusts.
The link between the appropriate advice to be taken and the Financial Services
and Markets Act 2000 is dealt with above. In addition, the trustees, or the fund
manager to whom a discretion has been delegated under section 34, must
exercise their investment powers with a view to giving effect to the principles
contained in the statement prepared pursuant to section 35 of the Pensions Act
1995. Failure to comply with section 36 exposes any trustee, who has failed to
take all reasonable steps to secure compliance, to the sanctions which can be
imposed by OPRA under sections 3 and 10 of the 1995 Act (see 11.7 above).

Employer-related investments

11.11   Section 40 of the Pensions Act 1995 restricts the extent to which
pension trustees may use their power of investment to invest in the business of
the employer. The reason for these provisions is that if a large proportion of
pension fund assets could be invested in that business, the fund would be
vulnerable if the employer became insolvent.

By section 40(1), pension trustees must secure that the scheme complies with
any prescribed regulations with respect to the proportion of its resources that
may at any time be invested in 'employer-related investments'. This expression
is defined in section 40(2) and includes the following types of investment:

- shares or other securities (not including government or other public
  securities – Pensions Act 1995, s 40(2A)) issued by the employer;

- land which is occupied or used by, or subject to a lease in favour of, the
  employer;

- property other than land which is used for the purposes of any business
  carried on by the employer;

- loans to the employer;

- any other prescribed investments.

In any of the above cases a person who is connected with, or an associate of, the
employer will also be covered by the section.

Regulation 5(1)(a) of the Occupational Pension Schemes (Investment) Regulations 1996 (SI 1996/3127) imposes a general limit of 5% of the current market
value of the resources of a scheme in respect of employer-related investments.
By regulation 5(1)(b), none of the resources of a scheme may at any time be
invested in any 'employer-related loan'. This term is defined in regulation 5(3)
and includes a loan falling within section 40(2)(d) of the 1995 Act.

By section 40(3), sums due and payable by a person to pension trustees are
regarded, to the extent they remain unpaid, as loans made to that person by the

trustees, and the resources of the scheme are regarded as invested accordingly. The effect of this is that unpaid contributions payable by the employer are regarded as employer-related investments.

Sanctions and penalties

11.12   As with sections 35 and 36, any trustee who fails to take all reasonable steps to secure compliance with the employer-related investments provisions may be the subject of sanctions under section 3 (prohibition order) or section 10 (civil penalty) of the Act. Moreover, if resources of a pension scheme are invested in contravention of section 40(1), a pension trustee who agreed in the determination to make the investment is guilty of an offence and is liable to a fine or imprisonment (Pensions Act 1995, s 40(5)). It would appear that a trustee can only be criminally liable under section 40(5) in respect of an active decision to invest as a result of which the scheme's employer-related investments exceed the prescribed restrictions. By contrast, sanctions could be imposed under sections 3 and 10 in respect of a failure by the trustees to remove scheme assets from employer-related investments if the restrictions began to be exceeded, for example following the acquisition by the employer of a company in which the scheme held shares.

Chapter 12

Charities

General principles

12.1   Detailed consideration was given to charitable trustees' exercise of their powers of investment in *Harries v Church Commissioners for England [1992] 1 WLR 1241*. In that case the claimants argued that the underlying purpose for which the commissioners held the fund's assets was the promotion of the Christian faith through the Church of England and that they were obliged to exercise their investment functions in accordance with this purpose, even where doing so involved a risk of significant financial detriment. They suggested that the commissioners should adopt a more 'ethical' investment policy. Nicholls V-C approached the duties of charitable trustees in relation to investment as a matter of principle in the absence of any directly relevant authority, holding that *Cowan v Scargill [1985] Ch 270* (see the discussion at 4.13) dealt with trusts whose object was to provide financial benefits for individuals.

In *Harries* it was held that the starting-point for charitable trustees in exercising their powers of investment did not differ from that for other trustees: they should seek to obtain the maximum return, whether by way of income or capital growth, consistent with commercial prudence. As Nicholls V-C said at p 1247:

> '... of their very nature, and by definition, investments are held by trustees to aid the work of the charity in a particular way: by generating money. That is the purpose for which they are held. That is their raison d'être'.

Exceptions to the basic principle

12.2   Nicholls V-C stated that there were circumstances in which charitable trustees might be permitted, or even obliged, to depart from this basic principle. He set out three particular situations, although stated that these were not exhaustive. One circumstance which would justify such a departure would be where holding investments of a particular type would conflict with the aims of the charity, such as a cancer research charity investing in tobacco companies. However, the existence of such a conflict would not normally mean that trustees would in fact be obliged to act to the detriment of their trusts: this would only be necessary if equally beneficial alternative investments were not available. Nicholls V-C considered that such circumstances would be unlikely to arise.

Secondly, trustees' holdings of particular investments might make potential recipients of aid unwilling to be helped, or might alienate the charity's financial supporters. While these situations are treated together in *Harries*, they are, in fact, quite distinct: in the first case the charity's ultimate aim would be hindered by the investment in question although its financial position would be unaffected, while in the second case the investment would risk the indirect effect of reducing the charity's funds. In either case, trustees might be justified in not making otherwise desirable investments where the difficulties or loss which would result would outweigh the financial detriment which the trust would suffer from not making the investment in question.

Thirdly, charitable trustees might be permitted or required to take non-financial criteria into account where the trust deed so provided; however, this exception is not peculiar to charitable trustees.

It was held, on the facts of the case, that the commissioners' policy of refraining from investing in companies whose main business was armaments, gambling, alcohol, tobacco or newspapers was justified on the basis that this left adequate scope for appropriately diverse investment which would not yield significantly less return to the trust fund. By contrast, the 'ethical' investment policy propounded by the claimants would financially disadvantage the fund. Their claim for declarations accordingly failed.

Application of the Trustee Act 2000

General powers

12.3   The general power of investment which is conferred on trustees by section 3 of the Trustee Act 2000 (as to which see generally 2.1) applies to charitable trusts in the same way as non-charitable ones. It can therefore be restricted or excluded in relation to a particular trust by a provision in the trust deed (Trustee Act 2000, s 6). The duty of care, which is imposed on trustees in relation to the exercise of their powers of investments by sections 1 and 2 of the Act, likewise applies to charitable trustees.

Power to employ agents

12.4   A distinction is, however, drawn between charitable and non-charitable trusts for the purposes of section 11 of the Act (power to employ agents). Non-charitable trustees may, by virtue of section 11(1) and (2), delegate any of their functions to an agent except those which are specifically set out in section 11(2); these are the functions which form the essence of the trustee's office, such as those relating to the way in which the fund is to be distributed.

Charitable trustees, by contrast, may *only* delegate those functions which are set out in section 11(3). Section 11(3)(a) provides that the trustees may delegate, as a general category, any function consisting of carrying out a decision that the trustees have taken. This provision, which does not give charitable trustees any powers of delegation over and above those they had before the 2000 Act, clearly does not allow the delegation of any function which involves the exercise of a discretion. However, provision is specifically made in section 11(3)(b) for delegation of any function relating to the investment of trust assets. This reflects the specialist nature of investment functions and the consequent undesirability of trustees being unable to delegate them to appropriately qualified professionals, which applies as much to charitable as to non-charitable trusts.

Parts II to IV of the Act, which contain the provisions relating to investment, acquisition of land, and agents, nominees and custodians respectively, do not apply to the following charitable trustees by virtue of section 38:

- generally, trustees managing a fund under a common investment scheme (as to which see 12.5 below);

- trustees managing a fund under a common deposit scheme (as to which see 12.12 below).

Common investment funds

12.5   Many charitable trust funds are, comparatively, very small. Consequently, it is often desirable for joint investment schemes to be established in order that the charities involved can benefit from the additional scope for diversification and the ability to share management and other fees which such schemes offer. However, the establishment of schemes of this nature generally involves the trustees in delegating their investment functions, which was not permitted before the coming into force of the Trustee Act 2000.

Certain individual common investment schemes were established by statutes such as the Universities and Colleges (Trusts) Act 1943, under which the Universities of Oxford and Cambridge, including the individual colleges within those universities, and Winchester College were enabled to establish schemes in order that their funds might be invested jointly. Moreover, it was held in *Re Royal Society's Charitable Trusts [1956] Ch 87* that the court had jurisdiction to sanction a scheme under which trustees of several charitable trust funds would be able to treat those trust funds as a single fund for the purposes of investment. However, the court stated that the jurisdiction should be exercised sparingly.

Statutory powers

12.6   The court and the Charity Commissioners were first given a general statutory power to make common investment schemes by section 22 of the Charities Act 1960. This provision has been largely re-enacted as section 24 of the Charities Act 1993. Under section 24(1) of the 1993 Act, the court or the

Commissioners may by order make and bring into effect schemes for the establishment of common investment funds under trusts which provide:

- for property transferred to the fund by or on behalf of a charity participating in the scheme to be invested under the control of trustees appointed to manage the fund; and

- for the participating charities to be entitled (subject to the provisions of the scheme) to the capital and income of the fund in shares determined by reference to the amount or value of the property transferred to it by or on behalf of each of them and to the value of the fund at the time of the transfers.

Requirements

12.7 A common investment scheme may be made on the application of any two or more charities (Charities Act 1993, s 24(2)). In *Re University of London Charitable Trusts [1964] Ch 282, 287* it was held that this requirement was satisfied if an application was made by the trustees of at least two charitable trusts even if they were the same persons. The scheme may be made in terms admitting any charity to participate, or it may restrict the right to participate in any manner (Charities Act 1993, s 24(3)).

By section 24(4) of the 1993 Act, a common investment scheme may make provision for, and for all matters connected with, the establishment, investment, management and winding up of the common investment fund. In particular, provision of the following sorts may be made:

- for remunerating persons appointed trustees to hold or manage the fund or any part of it, with or without provision authorising a person to receive the remuneration notwithstanding that he is also a charity trustee of or trustee for a participating charity;

- for restricting the size of the fund, and for regulating as to time, amount or otherwise the right to transfer property to or withdraw it from the fund, and for enabling sums to be advanced out of the fund by way of loan to a participating charity pending the withdrawal of property from the fund by the charity;

- for enabling income to be withheld from distribution with a view to avoiding fluctuations in the amounts distributed, and generally for regulating distributions of income;

- for enabling money to be borrowed temporarily for the purpose of meeting payments to be made out of the funds;

- for enabling questions arising under the scheme as to the right of a charity to participate, or as to the rights of participating charities, or as to any other matter, to be conclusively determined by the decision of the trustees managing the fund or in any other manner;

- for regulating the accounts and information to be supplied to participating charities.

Provision to allow charities a share of the fund

12.8   In addition to the provision for property to be transferred to the common investment fund on the basis that the charity is entitled to a share in the capital and income of the fund, the scheme may include provisions for enabling sums to be deposited by or on behalf of a charity on the basis (subject to the provisions of the scheme) that the charity shall be entitled to repayment of the sums deposited and to interest on those sums at a rate determined by or under the provisions of the scheme. Where a scheme makes such provision, it must also provide for excluding from the amount of capital and income to be shared between charities who are participating otherwise than by way of deposit such amounts as are required in respect of the liabilities of the fund for the repayment of deposits and interest on them, including amounts required by way of reserve (Charities Act 1993, s 24(5)).

Charities' rights may not be assigned

12.9   Section 24(6) of the Charities Act 1993 provides that the rights of a participating charity under a common investment scheme are not capable of being assigned or charged; and that no trustee or other person concerned in the management of the common investment fund shall be required or entitled to take account of any trust or other equity affecting a participating charity or its property or rights.

The powers of investment of every charity include power to participate in common investment schemes unless the power is excluded by a provision specifically referring to common investment schemes in the trusts of the charity (Charities Act 1993, s 24(7)).

Exempt charities

12.10   By virtue of section 24(8) of the 1993 Act, a common investment fund is deemed for all purposes to be a charity. Likewise, if only exempt charities are admitted to the scheme the fund is an exempt charity for the purposes of the 1993 Act. (Exempt charities are those set out in Schedule 2 to the Charities Act 1993. An exempt charity is not required to be registered by virtue of section 3(5) of the 1993 Act.)

This provision applies not only to common investment funds established under section 24 of the 1993 Act, but also to any similar fund established for the exclusive benefit of charities by or under any enactment relating to any particular charities or class of charity (Charities Act 1993, s 24(9)).

Other provisions

12.11   As noted at 12.4 above, Parts II to IV of the Trustee Act 2000 (which relate to investment, acquisition of land and agents, nominees and custodians respectively) do not generally apply to trustees managing a fund under a common investment scheme (Trustee Act 2000, s 38(1)). However, these provisions will apply where the trusts of the fund provide that property is not to be transferred to it except by a charity of which the trustees are those appointed to manage the fund itself.

Thus trustees of a common investment fund of the sort established in *Re Royal Society's Charitable Trusts [1956] Ch 87* (see 12.5 above), who are also the trustees of all the trusts making up the fund, will be able to delegate their powers under the relevant provisions of the 2000 Act. The reasoning behind this exception is that the establishment of the common investment fund in such a case will not itself have involved the trustees in delegating their investment powers.

Common deposit schemes

12.12   An alternative to the establishment of a common investment fund is the making of a common deposit scheme under section 25 of the Charities Act 1993, which unlike section 24 was not a re-enactment of a provision in the Charities Act 1960.

By virtue of section 25(1) the court or the Commissioners may make schemes for the establishment of common deposit funds under trusts which provide for sums to be deposited by or on behalf of a charity participating in the scheme and, as in the case of common investment funds, invested under the control of trustees appointed to manage the fund. Rather than the participating charities being entitled to *aliquot* shares of the income and capital in the fund, each charity is entitled (subject to the provisions of the scheme) to repayment of any sums deposited and to interest on them at a rate determined under the scheme. With the exception of certain variations set out in section 25(3) of the 1993 Act, subsections (2) to (4) and (6) to (9) of section 24 have effect in relation to common deposit scheme funds as they have effect in relation to common investment schemes and funds (Charities Act 1993, s 25(2)).

It will be seen that section 24(5) of the Charities Act 1993 (as to which see 12.8 above) effectively provides the establishment of schemes combining the elements of common investment schemes and common deposit schemes.

As noted at 12.11 above, Parts II to IV of the Trustee Act 2000 do not apply to trustees managing a fund under a common deposit scheme (Trustee Act 2000, s 38(2)).

Appendices

Contents

Appendix 1

Draft Policy Statement and Appointment of Investment Manager

App 1.1

DRAFT POLICY STATEMENT AND APPOINTMENT OF INVESTMENT MANAGER UNDER SECTION 15(2)(a) TRUSTEE ACT 2000

Particulars of the settlement:

Date:
Trustees:
Trust powers of investment: see Schedule 1

Proposed investment manager:

Firm name:
Investment manager / contact name:
Contact details:
E-mail
Telephone
Fax
Postal address

Policy statement:

The terms of the proposed investment manager's agreement annexed apply except insofar as they are inconsistent with the terms set out in this Statement, when this Statement shall prevail.

The authority to deal:

This appointment of the investment manager authorises purchases and sales of investments on behalf of the trustees without previous reference to them in connection with the funds of this Settlement.

The authority to select investments:

Within the scope of the powers of investment set out in Schedule 1 and subject to the duties placed on trustees in selecting investments by the general law and to what is stated below, the investment manager is authorised to purchase stocks and shares throughout the world and units in all unit trusts and offshore funds, including unit trusts under the management of the investment manager.

Exceptions to the authority:

The investment manager may not sell any investments that are listed in Schedule 2 Part 1. without our specific authority.

The investment manager may not invest in any investments of the type listed in Schedule 2 Part 2, in which the trustees do not wish to invest.

The trustees will give the investment manager notice of any change in either of these categories of investment.

Overall investment policy:

The trustees recognise a duty under the general law to have regard to the interests of all beneficiaries, both present and future, and whether in capital or income. Subject to that, Schedule 3 sets out the balance between income and capital growth which the trustees consider appropriate to the circumstances of the Settlement.

Review:

The trustees require the investment manager to produce valuations of the investments in the Settlement and reports on the portfolio:

(i) at least [every   months] and

[(ii) at the end of any calendar month during which when the principal market in which the fund is invested has moved in value by more than [%] of its value at the beginning of that month.]

The Trustees will indicate any change in overall investment policy from time to time.

Cash:

Any cash forming part of the portfolio which is not immediately required for the purpose of any transactions may be placed on deposit in any currency at normal commercial rates of interest. Small balances of less than [£......] may temporarily be held on current account.

Duty of care:

In managing the portfolio as delegates of the trustees, the investment manager must assume the duty of care to the beneficiaries of the trustees without limitation save as below. The investment manager's liability for loss caused by negligence or otherwise on its part or on the part of any of its staff will be the same as, but no greater than, the liability of the trustees to all or any of the beneficiaries of the Settlement for any breach of trust involved in any act or default on the part of the investment manager or of its staff. Any such liability is to be joint and several and must include any liability by way of interest or costs.

Liquidity:

The trustees expect to need to realise capital from the fund in accordance with Schedule 4.

Residence and tax status of trust:

[set out details.]

Fees:

The trustees agree to pay service charges (plus VAT where appropriate) in accordance with the investment manager's current scale of stated charges as amended from time to time by prior written notice, which may be deducted from any cash balances held by the investment manager.

SCHEDULE 1

[The general power of investment under section 3 Trustee Act 2000]
or
Powers set out in the [....................] settlement: [copied from the trust instrument]

SCHEDULE 2

PART 1
The following holdings must not be sold without the prior consent of the trustees:

PART 2
No holdings may be bought in the following companies or sectors without the prior consent of the trustees: [eg ethical considerations]

SCHEDULE 3

Subject as below, the investment policy for this account is to be based on an even balance between income and capital growth.

Level of return of income required: [eg at least as good as Financial Times Private investor's index for an Income portfolio]

Overall return sought:

Proportion of fund to be invested in:

[Residential property]
[Commercial property]
[Farmland]
[Woodland]
[UK fixed interest]
[UK equity]
[UK derivatives]
[Non-UK fixed interest]
[Non-UK equity]
[Works of art]
[Other]

SCHEDULE 4

Capital will be required from the fund in the future as follows:

117

[eg, (i) IHT on death of tenant for life, now aged . . ., estimated at . . .% of the then value of the fund

(ii) attainder of a vested interest in A&M trust – dates and names and shares

(iii) CGT on occasion that a beneficiary becomes absolutely entitled.]

This draft was produced by:
C R T Harris LLB CTA TEP
Chartered Tax Adviser
Registered Trust & Estate Practitioner

Appendix 2

Statutory Provisions

App 2.1

Trustee Investments Act 1961

1 New powers of investment of trustees

(1) A trustee may invest any property in his hands, whether at the time in a state of investment or not, in any manner specified in Part I or II of the First Schedule to this Act or, subject to the next following section, in any manner specified in Part III of that Schedule, and may also from time to time vary any such investments.

(2) The supplemental provisions contained in Part IV of that Schedule shall have effect for the interpretation and for restricting the operation of the said Parts I to III.

(3) No provision relating to the powers of the trustee contained in any instrument (not being an enactment or an instrument made under an enactment) made before the passing of this Act shall limit the powers conferred by this section, but those powers are exerciseable only in so far as a contrary intention is not expressed in any Act or instrument made under an enactment, whenever passed or made, and so relating or in any other instrument so relating which is made after the passing of this Act.

For the purposes of this subsection any rule of the law of Scotland whereby a testamentary writing may be deemed to be made on a date other than that on which it was actually executed shall be disregarded.

(4) In this Act "narrower-range investment" means an investment falling within Part I or II of the First Schedule to this Act and "wider-range investment" means an investment falling within Part III of that Schedule.

NOTES

Amendment
Repealed, except in so far as this section is applied by or under any other enactment, by the Trustee Act 2000, s 40(1), (3), Sch 2, Pt I, para 1(1), Sch 4, Pt I.
  Date in force: 1 February 2001: see SI 2001/49, art 2.

2   Restrictions on wider-range investment

(1) A trustee shall not have power by virtue of the foregoing section to make or retain any wider-range investment unless the trust fund has been divided into two parts (hereinafter referred to as the narrower-range part and the wider-range part), the parts being, subject to the provisions of this Act, equal in value at the time of the division; and where such a division has been made no subsequent division of the same fund shall be made for the purposes of this section, and no property shall be transferred from one part of the fund to the other unless either—

>   (a)   the transfer is authorised or required by the following provisions of this Act, or

>   (b)   a compensating transfer is made at the same time.

In this section "compensating transfer", in relation to any transferred property, means a transfer in the opposite direction of property of equal value.

(2) Property belonging to the narrower-range part of a trust fund shall not by virtue of the foregoing section be invested except in narrower-range investments, and any property invested in any other manner which is or becomes comprised in that part of the trust fund shall either be transferred to the wider-range part of the fund, with a compensating transfer, or be reinvested in narrower-range investments as soon as may be.

(3) Where any property accrues to a trust fund after the fund has been divided in pursuance of subsection (1) of this section, then—

>   (a)   if the property accrues to the trustee as owner or former owner of property comprised in either part of the fund, it shall be treated as belonging to that part of the fund;

>   (b)   in any other case, the trustee shall secure, by apportionment of the accruing property or the transfer of property from one part of the fund to the other, or both, that the value of each part of the fund is increased by the same amount.

Where a trustee acquires property in consideration of a money payment the acquisition of the property shall be treated for the purposes of this section as investment and not as the accrual of property to the trust fund, notwithstanding that the amount of the consideration is less than the value of the property acquired; and paragraph (a) of this subsection shall not include the case of a dividend or interest becoming part of a trust fund.

(4) Where in the exercise of any power or duty of a trustee property falls to be taken out of the trust fund, nothing in this section shall restrict his discretion as to the choice of property to be taken out.

NOTES

Amendment
Repealed, except in so far as this section is applied by or under any other enactment,
by the Trustee Act 2000, s 40(1), (3), Sch 2, Pt I, para 1(1), Sch 4, Pt I.

Date in force: 1 February 2001: see SI 2001/49, art 2.

3   Relationship between Act and other powers of investment

(1) The powers conferred by section one of this Act are in addition to and not in derogation from any power conferred otherwise than by this Act of investment or postponing conversion exerciseable by a trustee (hereinafter referred to as a "special power").

(2) Any special power (however expressed) to invest property in any investment for the time being authorised by law for the investment of trust property, being a power conferred on a trustee before the passing of this Act or conferred on him under any enactment passed before the passing of this Act, shall have effect as a power to invest property in like manner and subject to the like provisions as under the foregoing provisions of this Act.

(3) In relation to property, including wider-range but not including narrower-range investments,—

   (a)   which a trustee is authorised to hold apart from—

      (i)   the provisions of section one of this Act or any of the provisions of Part I of the Trustee Act 1925, or any of the provisions of the Trusts (Scotland) Act 1921, or

      (ii)   any such power to invest in authorised investments as is mentioned in the foregoing subsection, or

   (b)   which became part of a trust fund in consequence of the exercise by the trustee, as owner of property falling within this subsection, of any power conferred by subsection (3) or (4) of section ten of the Trustee Act 1925, or paragraph (o) or (p) of subsection (1) of section four of the Trusts (Scotland) Act 1921,
the foregoing section shall have effect subject to the modifications set out in the Second Schedule to this Act.

(4) The foregoing subsection shall not apply where the powers of the trustee to invest or postpone conversion have been conferred or varied—

   (a)   by an order of any court made within the period of ten years ending with the passing of this Act, or

   (b)   by any enactment passed, or instrument having effect under an enactment made, within that period, being an enactment or instrument relating specifically to the trusts in question; or

   (c)   by an enactment contained in a local Act of the present Session;
but the provisions of the Third Schedule to this Act shall have effect in a case falling within this subsection.

NOTES

Amendment
Repealed, except in so far as this section relates to a trustee having a power of investment conferred on him under any enactment which was passed before 3 August

1961 and which is not amended by the Trustee Act 2000, Sch 2, by the Trustee Act 2000, s 40(1), (3), Sch 2, Pt I, para 1(2), Sch 4, Pt I.
  Date in force: 1 February 2001: see SI 2001/49, art 2.

4   Interpretation of references to trust property and trust funds

(1) In this Act "property" includes real or personal property of any description, including money and things in action:

Provided that it does not include an interest in expectancy, but the falling into possession of such an interest, or the receipt of proceeds of the sale thereof, shall be treated for the purposes of this Act as an accrual of property to the trust fund.

(2) So much of the property in the hands of a trustee shall for the purposes of this Act constitute one trust fund as is held on trusts which (as respects the beneficiaries or their respective interests or the purposes of the trust or as respects the powers of the trustee) are not identical with those on which any other property in his hands is held.

(3) Where property is taken out of a trust fund by way of appropriation so as to form a separate fund, and at the time of the appropriation the trust fund had (as to the whole or a part thereof) been divided in pursuance of subsection (1) of section two of this Act, or that subsection as modified by the Second Schedule to this Act, then if the separate fund is so divided the narrower-range and wider-range parts of the separate fund may be constituted so as either to be equal, or to bear to each other the same proportion as the two corresponding parts of the fund out of which it was so appropriated (the values of those parts of those funds being ascertained as at the time of appropriation), or some intermediate proportion.

(4) …

NOTES
Sub-s (4): applies to Scotland only.

5   Certain valuations to be conclusive for purposes of division of trust fund

(1) If for the purposes of section two or four of this Act or the Second Schedule thereto a trustee obtains, from a person reasonably believed by the trustee to be qualified to make it, a valuation in writing of any property, the valuation shall be conclusive in determining whether the division of the trust fund in pursuance of subsection (1) of the said section two, or any transfer or apportionment of property under that section or the said Second Schedule, has been duly made.

(2) The foregoing subsection applies to any such valuation notwithstanding that it is made by a person in the course of his employment as an officer or servant.

NOTES

Amendment
Repealed, except in so far as this section is applied by or under any other enactment,
by the Trustee Act 2000, s 40(1), (3), Sch 2, Pt I, para 1(1), Sch 4, Pt I.
  Date in force: 1 February 2001: see SI 2001/49, art 2.

6 Duty of trustees in choosing investments

(1) In the exercise of his powers of investment a trustee shall have regard—

  (a)   to the need for diversification of investments of the trust, in so far
      as is appropriate to the circumstances of the trust;

  (b)   to the suitability to the trust of investments of the description of
      investment proposed and of the investment proposed as an invest-
      ment of that description.

(2) Before exercising any power conferred by section one of this Act to invest
a manner specified in Part II or III of the First Schedule to this Act, or before
investing in any such manner in the exercise of a power falling within
subsection (2) of section three of this Act, a trustee shall obtain and consider
proper advice on the question whether the investment is satisfactory having
regard to the matters mentioned in paragraphs (a) and (b) of the foregoing
subsection.

(3) A trustee retaining any investment made in the exercise of such a power
and in such a manner as aforesaid shall determine at what intervals the
circumstances, and in particular the nature of the investment, make it
desirable to obtain such advice as aforesaid, and shall obtain and consider
such advice accordingly.

(4) For the purposes of the two foregoing subsections, proper advice is the
advice of a person who is reasonably believed by the trustee to be qualified by
his ability in and practical experience of financial matters; and such advice
may be given by a person notwithstanding that he gives it in the course of his
employment as an officer or servant.

(5) A trustee shall not be treated as having complied with subsection (2) or
(3) of this section unless the advice was given or has been subsequently
confirmed in writing.

(6) Subsections (2) and (3) of this section shall not apply to one of two or
more trustees where he is the person giving the advice required by this section
to his co-trustee or co-trustees, and shall not apply where powers of a trustee
are lawfully exercised by an officer or servant competent under subsection (4)
of this section to give proper advice.

(7) Without prejudice to section eight of the Trustee Act 1925, or section
thirty of the Trusts (Scotland) Act 1921 (which relate to valuation, and the
proportion of the value to be lent, where a trustee lends on the security of
property) the advice required by this section shall not include, in the case of a

loan on the security of freehold or leasehold property in England and Wales or Northern Ireland or on heritable security in Scotland, advice on the suitability of the particular loan.

NOTES

Amendment
Repealed, except in so far as this section is applied by or under any other enactment, by the Trustee Act 2000, s 40(1), (3), Sch 2, Pt I, para 1(1), Sch 4, Pt I.
Date in force: 1 February 2001: see SI 2001/49, art 2.

7 Application of ss 1–6 to persons, other than trustees, having trustee investment powers

(1) Where any persons, not being trustees, have a statutory power of making investments which is or includes power—

(a) to make the like investments as are authorised by section one of the Trustee Act 1925, or section ten of the Trusts (Scotland) Act 1921, or

(b) to make the like investments as trustees are for the time being by law authorised to make,

however the power is expressed, the foregoing provisions of this Act shall with the necessary modifications apply in relation to them as if they were trustees:

Provided that property belonging to a Consolidated Loans Fund or any other fund applicable wholly or partly for the redemption of debt shall not by virtue of the foregoing provisions of this Act be invested or held invested in any manner specified in paragraph 6 of Part II of the First Schedule to this Act or in wider-range investments.

(2) Where, in the exercise of powers conferred by any enactment, an authority to which paragraph 9 of Part II of the First Schedule to this Act applies uses money belonging to any fund for a purpose for which the authority has power to borrow, the foregoing provisions of this Act, as applied by the foregoing subsection, shall apply as if there were comprised in the fund (in addition to the actual content thereof) property, being narrower-range investments, having a value equal to so much of the said money as for the time being has not been repaid to the fund, and accordingly any repayment of such money to the fund shall not be treated for the said purposes as the accrual of property to the fund:

Provided that nothing in this subsection shall be taken to require compliance with any of the provisions of section six of this Act in relation to the exercise of such powers as aforesaid.

(3) In this section "Consolidated Loans Fund" means a fund established under section fifty-five of the Local Government Act 1958, and includes a loans fund established under section two hundred and seventy-five of the Local Government (Scotland) Act 1947, and "statutory power" means a

power conferred by an enactment passed before the passing of this Act or by any instrument made under any such enactment.

8 ...

...

NOTES

Amendment
Repealed by the Trustee Act 2000, s 40(1), (3), Sch 2, Pt I, para 1(3)(a), Sch 4, Pt I.
Date in force: 1 February 2001: see SI 2001/49, art 2.

9 ...

...

NOTES

Amendment
Repealed by the Trustee Act 2000, s 40(1), (3), Sch 2, Pt I, para 1(3)(a), Sch 4, Pt I.
Date in force: 1 February 2001: see SI 2001/49, art 2.

11   Local Authority investment schemes

(1) Without prejudice to powers conferred by or under any other enactment, any authority to which this section applies may invest property held by the authority in accordance with a scheme submitted to the Treasury by any association of local authorities ... and approved by the Treasury as enabling investments to be made collectively without in substance extending the scope of powers of investment.

(2) A scheme under this section may apply to a specified authority or to a specified class of authorities, may make different provisions as respects different authorities or different classes of authorities or as respects different descriptions of property or property held for different purposes, and may impose restrictions on the extent to which the power controlled by the foregoing subsection shall be exerciseable.

(3) In approving a scheme under this section, the Treasury may direct that [the Financial Services Act 1986], shall not apply to dealings undertaken or documents issued for the purposes of the scheme, or to such dealings or documents of such descriptions as may be specified in the direction.

(4) The authorities to which this section applies are—

> (a)   in England and Wales[, the Greater London Authority,] the council of a county, [a county borough,] a ... borough ... a district or a [parish, the Common] Council of the City of London[, a functional body (within the meaning of the Greater

London Authority Act 1999),] [the Broads Authority] [a National Park authority][, a police authority established under [section 3 of the Police Act 1996]][, the Service Authority for the National Crime Squad][, ... a joint authority established by Part IV of the Local Government Act 1985] ... and the Council of the Isles of Scilly;

(b)   in Scotland, a local authority within the meaning of the Local Government (Scotland) Act 1947;

(c)   in any part of Great Britain, a joint board or joint committee constituted to discharge or advise on the discharge of the functions of any two or more of the authorities mentioned in the foregoing paragraphs (including a joint committee established by [those authorities acting in combination in accordance with regulations made under section 7 of the Superannuation Act 1972];

(d)   in Northern Ireland, [a district council established under the Local Government Act (Northern Ireland) 1972] and the Northern Ireland Local Government Officers' Superannuation Committee established under the Local Government (Superannuation) Act (Northern Ireland) 1950;

[(e)   in any part of the United Kingdom, the Service Authority for the National Criminal Intelligence Service.]

NOTES

Initial Commencement

Royal Assent
Royal Assent: 3 August 1961: (no specific commencement provision).
Amendment
Sub-s (1): words omitted repealed by the London Government Act 1963, s 93(1), Sch 8, Pt II and by the Local Government Act 1985, s 102, Sch 17.
   Sub-s (3): words in square brackets beginning with the word "the" substituted by the Financial Services Act 1986, s 212(2), Sch 16, para 2.
   Sub-s (3): words "Financial Services and Markets Act 2000" in square brackets substituted by SI 2001/3649, art 268.
   Date in force: 1 December 2001: see SI 2001/3649, art 1.
   Sub-s (4): in para (a) words ", the Greater London Authority," in square brackets inserted by the Greater London Authority Act 1999, s 387(1), (2)(a).
   Date in force (for the purposes of its application to the Greater London Authority): 8 May 2000: see SI 1999/3434, art 3.
   Date in force (for remaining purposes): 3 July 2000: see SI 1999/3434, art 4.
   Sub-s (4): in para (a) words "a county borough," in square brackets inserted by the Local Government (Wales) Act 1994, s 66(6), Sch 16, para 19(1).
   Sub-s (4): in para (a) first words omitted repealed by the London Government Act 1963, s 93(1), Sch 18, Pt II.
   Sub-s (4): in para (a) second words omitted repealed by the Local Government Act 1972, s 272(1), Sch 30.
   Sub-s (4): in para (a) words "parish, the Common" in square brackets substituted by the Water Act 1989, s 190, Sch 25, para 29.

Sub-s (4): in para (a) words ", a functional body (within the meaning of the Greater London Authority Act 1999)," in square brackets inserted by the Greater London Authority Act 1999, s 387(1), (2)(b).

Date in force (for the purposes of its application to the Greater London Authority): 8 May 2000: see SI 1999/3434, art 3.

Date in force (for remaining purposes): 3 July 2000: see SI 1999/3434, art 4.

Sub-s (4): in para (a) words "the Broads Authority" in square brackets inserted by the Norfolk and Suffolk Broads Act 1988, s 21, Sch 6.

Sub-s (4): in para (a) words "a National Park authority" in square brackets inserted by the Environment Act 1995, s 78, Sch 10, para 5.

Sub-s (4): in para (a) words in square brackets beginning with the words ", a police authority" inserted by the Police and Magistrates' Courts Act 1994, s 43, Sch 4, Pt II, para 46.

Sub-s (4): in para (a) words "section 3 of the Police Act 1996" in square brackets substituted by the Police Act 1996, s 103, Sch 7, para 1(2)(a).

Sub-s (4): in para (a) words ", the Service Authority for the National Crime Squad" in square brackets inserted by the Police Act 1997, s 134(1), Sch 9, para 4(a).

Date in force: 1 April 1998: see SI 1998/354, art 2(2)(bb).

Sub-s (4): in para (a) words in square brackets ending with the words "Local Government Act 1985" inserted by the Local Government Act 1985, s 84, Sch 14, para 38.

Sub-s (4): in para (a) third words omitted repealed by the Education Reform Act 1988, s 237, Sch 13, Pt I.

Sub-s (4): in para (a) fourth words omitted repealed by the Local Government Act 1985, s 102, Sch 17.

Sub-s (4): in para (c) words from "those authorities" to "Act 1972" in square brackets substituted by the Superannuation Act 1972, s 29(1), Sch 6, para 40.

Sub-s (4): in para (d) words from "a district" to "Ireland) 1972" in square brackets substituted by the Transfer of Functions (Local Government, etc) (Northern Ireland) Order 1973, SR & O 1973/256, art 3, Sch 2.

Sub-s (4): para (e) inserted by the Police Act 1997, s 134(1), Sch 9, para 4(b).

Date in force: 1 April 1998: see SI 1998/354, art 2(2)(bb).

Modification

Modified by the Waste Regulation and Disposal (Authorities) Order 1985, SI 1985/1884, art 10, Sch 3.

See Further

See further, for provision whereby the body corporate known as the Residuary Body for Wales is to be included among the authorities or bodies to which this section applies: the Local Government (Wales) Act 1994, Sch 13, para 24(a).

12   Power to confer additional powers of investment

(1) Her Majesty may by Order in Council extend the powers of investment conferred by section one of this Act by adding to Part I, Part II or Part III of the First Schedule to this Act any manner of investment specified in the Order.

(2) Any Order under this section shall be subject to annulment in pursuance of a resolution of either House of Parliament.

NOTES

Amendment

Repealed, except in so far as this section is applied by or under any other enactment, by the Trustee Act 2000, s 40(1), (3), Sch 2, Pt I, para 1(1), Sch 4, Pt I.

Date in force: 1 February 2001: see SI 2001/49, art 2.

13 Power to modify provisions as to division of trust fund

(1) The Treasury may by order made by statutory instrument direct that, subject to subsection (3) of section four of this Act, any division of a trust fund made in pursuance of subsection (1) of section two of this Act during the continuance in force of the order shall be made so that the value of the wider-range part at the time of the division bears to the then value of the narrower- range part such proportion, greater than one but not greater than three to one, as may be prescribed by the order; and in this Act "the prescribed proportion" means the proportion for the time being prescribed under this subsection.

(2) A fund which has been divided in pursuance of subsection (1) of section two of this Act before the coming into operation of an order under the foregoing subsection may notwithstanding anything in that subsection be again divided (once only) in pursuance of the said subsection (1) during the continuance in force of the order.

(3) If an order is made under subsection (1) of this section, then as from the coming into operation of the order—

    (a)   paragraph (b) of subsection (3) of section two of this Act and sub-paragraph (b) of paragraph 3 of the Second Schedule thereto shall have effect with the substitution, for the words from "each" to the end, of the words "the wider-range part of the fund is increased by an amount which bears the prescribed proportion to the amount by which the value of the narrower-range part of the fund is increased";

    (b)   subsection (3) of section four of this Act shall have effect as if for the words "so as either" to "each other" there were substituted the words "so as to bear to each other either the prescribed proportion or".

(4) An order under this section may be revoked by a subsequent order thereunder prescribing a greater proportion.

(5) An order under this section shall not have effect unless approved by a resolution of each House of Parliament.

NOTES
Amendment
Repealed, except in so far as this section is applied by or under any other enactment, by the Trustee Act 2000, s 40(1), (3), Sch 2, Pt I, para 1(1), Sch 4, Pt I.
    Date in force: 1 February 2001: see SI 2001/49, art 2.

15 Saving for powers of court

The enlargement of the investment powers of trustees by this Act shall not lessen any power of a court to confer wider powers of investment on trustees, or affect the extent to which any such power is to be exercised.

NOTES

Amendment
Repealed, except in so far as this section is applied by or under any other enactment,
by the Trustee Act 2000, s 40(1), (3), Sch 2, Pt I, para 1(1), Sch 4, Pt I.
  Date in force: 1 February 2001: see SI 2001/49, art 2.

16 Minor and consequential amendments and repeals

(1) The provisions of the Fourth Schedule to this Act (which contain minor
amendments and amendments consequential on the foregoing provisions of
this Act) shall have effect.

(2) < ... >

NOTES

Initial Commencement

Royal Assent
Royal Assent: 3 August 1961: (no specific commencement provision).

Amendment
Sub-s (1): repealed, in so far as it relates to Sch 4, para 1(1), by the Trustee Act 2000,
s 40(1), (3), Sch 2, Pt I, para 1(3)(c), Sch 4, Pt I.
  Date in force: 1 February 2001: see SI 2001/49, art 2.
Sub-s (2): repealed by the Statute Law (Repeals) Act 1974.

17 Short title, extent and construction

(1) This Act may be cited as the Trustee Investments Act 1961.

(2) Sections eleven and sixteen of this Act shall extend to Northern Ireland,
but except as aforesaid and except so far as any other provisions of the Act
apply by virtue of subsection (1) of section one of the Trustee Act (Northern
Ireland) 1958, or any other enactment of the Parliament of Northern Ireland,
to trusts the execution of which is governed by the law in force in Northern
Ireland, this Act does not apply to such trusts.

(3) So much of section sixteen of this Act as relates to [the National Savings
Bank] ... shall extend to the Isle of Man and the Channel Islands.

(4) Except where the context otherwise requires, in this Act, in its application
to trusts the execution of which is governed by the law in force in England
and Wales, expressions have the same meaning as in the Trustee Act 1925.

(5) ...

NOTES

Amendment
Sub-s (3): words in square brackets substituted by the Post Office Act 1969, ss 94, 114,
Sch 6, Part III; words omitted repealed by the Trustee Savings Banks Act 1985, ss 4(3),
7(3), Sch 4.

Sub-s (5): applies to Scotland only.
Modification
The Northern Ireland Act 1998 makes new provision for the government of Northern Ireland for the purpose of implementing the Belfast Agreement (the agreement reached at multi-party talks on Northern Ireland and set out in Command Paper 3883). As a consequence of that Act, any reference in this section to the Parliament of Northern Ireland or the Assembly established under the Northern Ireland Assembly Act 1973, s 1, certain office-holders and Ministers, and any legislative act and certain financial dealings thereof, shall, for the period specified, be construed in accordance with Sch 12, paras 1–11 to the 1998 Act.

SCHEDULE 1 (SECTION 1)
MANNER OF INVESTMENT

Part I Narrower-Range Investments not Requiring Advice

1 In Defence Bonds, National Savings Certificates Ulster Savings Certificates, [Ulster Development Bonds] [National Development Bonds], [British Savings Bonds], [National Savings Income Bonds] [National Savings Deposit Bonds] [National Savings Indexed-Income Bonds], [National Savings Capital Bonds] [National Savings FIRST Option Bonds], [National Savings Pensioners Guaranteed Income Bonds].

2 In deposits in [the National Savings Bank], ... and deposits in a bank or department thereof certified under subsection (3) of section nine of the Finance Act 1956.

NOTES
Amendment
Repealed, except in so far as this Schedule is applied by or under any other enactment, by virtue of the Trustee Act 2000, s 40(1), (3), Sch 2, Pt I, para 1(1), Sch 4, Pt I.

Part II Narrower-Range of Investments Requiring Advice

1 In securities issued by Her Majesty's Government in the United Kingdom, the Government of Northern Ireland or the Government of the Isle of Man, not being securities falling within Part I of this Schedule and being fixed-interest securities registered in the United Kingdom or the Isle of Man, Treasury Bills or Tax Reserve Certificates [or any variable interest securities issued by Her Majesty's Government in the United Kingdom and registered in the United Kingdom].

2 In any securities the payment of interest on which is guaranteed by Her Majesty's Government in the United Kingdom or the Government of Northern Ireland.

3 In fixed-interest securities issued in the United Kingdom by any public authority or nationalised industry or undertaking in the United Kingdom.

4 In fixed-interest securities issued in the United Kingdom by the government of any overseas territory within the Commonwealth or by any public or local authority within such a territory, being securities registered in the United Kingdom.

References in this paragraph to an overseas territory or to the government of such a territory shall be construed as if they occurred in the Overseas Service Act, 1958.

[4A In securities issued in the United Kingdom by the government of an overseas territory within the Commonwealth or by any public or local authority within such a territory, being securities registered in the United Kingdom and in respect of which the rate of interest is variable by reference to one or more of the following:—

   (a)   the Bank of England's minimum lending rate;

   (b)   the average rate of discount on allotment on 91-day Treasury bills;

   (c)   a yield on 91-day Treasury bills;

   (d)   a London sterling inter-bank offered rate;

   (e)   a London sterling certificate of deposit rate.

References in this paragraph to an overseas territory or to the government of such a territory shall be construed as if they occurred in the Overseas Service Act 1958.]

5 In fixed-interest securities issued in the United Kingdom by [the African Development Bank, the Asian Development Bank, the Caribbean Development Bank, [the European Bank for Reconstruction and Development,] the International Finance Corporation, the International Monetary Fund or by] the International Bank for Reconstruction and Development, being securities registered in the United Kingdom.

[In fixed-interest securities issued in the United Kingdom by the Inter-American Development Bank],

[In fixed interest securities issued in the United Kingdom by [the European Atomic Energy Community, the European Economic Community,] the European Investment Bank or by the European Coal and Steel Community, being securities registered in the United Kingdom.]

[5A In securities issued in the United Kingdom by

   (i)   the International Bank for Reconstruction and Development or by the European Investment Bank or by the European Coal and Steel Community, being securities registered in the United Kingdom or

   (ii)   the Inter-American Development Bank
being securities in respect of which the rate of interest is variable by reference to one or more of the following:—

   (a)   the Bank of England's minimum lending rate;

(b)   the average rate of discount on allotment on 91-day Treasury bills;

(c)   a yield on 91-day Treasury bills;

(d)   a London sterling inter-bank offered rate;

(e)   a London sterling certificate of deposit rate.]

[**5B** In securities issued in the United Kingdom by the African Development Bank, the Asian Development Bank, the Caribbean Development Bank, the European Atomic Energy Community, [the European Bank for Reconstruction and Development,] the European Economic Community, the International Finance Corporation or by the International Monetary Fund, being securities registered in the United Kingdom and in respect of which the rate of interest is variable by reference to one or more of the following:—

(a)   The average rate of discount on allotment on 91-day Treasury Bills;

(b)   a yield on 91-day Treasury Bills;

(c)   a London sterling inter-bank offered rate;

(d)   a London sterling certificate of deposit rate.]

6 In debentures issued in the United Kingdom by a company incorporated in the United Kingdom, being debentures registered in the United Kingdom.

7 In stock of the Bank of Ireland.

[In Bank of Ireland 7 per cent. Loan Stock 1968/91].

8

...

9 In loans to any authority to which this paragraph applies charged on all or any of the revenues of the authority or on a fund into which all or any of those revenues are payable, in any fixed-interest securities issued in the United Kingdom by any such authority for the purpose of borrowing money so charged, and in deposits with any such authority by way of temporary loan made on the giving of a receipt for the loan by the treasurer or other similar officer of the authority and on the giving of an undertaking by the authority that, if requested to charge the loan as aforesaid, it will either comply with the request or repay the loan.

This paragraph applies to the following authorities, that is to say—

(a)   any local authority in the United Kingdom;

[(aa) the Greater London Authority;

(ab) any functional body, within the meaning of the Greater London Authority Act 1999;]

(b)   any authority all the members of which are appointed or elected by one or more local authorities in the United Kingdom;

(c)   any authority the majority of the members of which are appointed or elected by one or more local authorities in the United Kingdom, being an authority which by virtue of any enactment has power to issue a precept to a local authority in England and Wales, or a requisition to a local authority in Scotland, or to the expenses of which, by virtue of any enactment, a local authority in the United Kingdom is or can be required to contribute;

(d)   ...[a police authority established under [section 3 of the Police Act 1996]];

[(da) the Service Authority for the National Criminal Intelligence Service or the Service Authority for the National Crime Squad;]

(e)   the Belfast City and District Water Commissioners;

[(f)   the Great Ouse Water Authority];

[(g)   any district council in Northern Ireland;]

[(h)   ... ;

(i)   any residuary body established by section 57 of the Local Government Act 1985.]

[**9A** In any securities issued in the United Kingdom by any authority to which paragraph 9 applies for the purpose of borrowing money charged on all or any of the revenues of the authority or on a fund into which all or any of those revenues are payable and being securities in respect of which the rate of interest is variable by reference to one or more of the following:—

(a)   the Bank of England's minimum lending rate;

(b)   the average rate of discount on allotment on 91-day Treasury bills;

(c)   a yield on 91-day Treasury bills;

(d)   a London sterling inter-bank offered rate;

(e)   a London sterling certificate of deposit rate.]

10

...

[**10A** In any units of a gilt unit trust scheme.

References in this Schedule to a gilt unit trust scheme are references to a collective investment scheme—

(a)   which is an authorised unit trust scheme within the meaning of the Financial Services Act 1986, a recognised scheme within the meaning of that Act or a UCITS; and

(b)   whose objective is to invest not less than 90% of the property of the scheme in loan stock, bonds and other instruments creating or acknowledging indebtedness which are transferable and which are issued or guaranteed by—

(i) the government of the United Kingdom [or of any other country or territory],

(ii) by a local authority in the United Kingdom or in a relevant state, or

(iii) by an international organisation the members of which include the United Kingdom or a relevant state;

and, in respect of the remainder of the property of the scheme, whose objective is to invest in any instrument falling within any of paragraphs 1 to 3, 5 or 6 of Schedule 1 to the Financial Services Act 1986.]

11

...

[**12** In deposits with a building society within the meaning of the Building Societies Act 1986.]

13 In mortgages of freehold property in England and Wales or Northern Ireland and of leasehold property in those countries of which the unexpired term at the time of investment is not less than sixty years, and in loans on heritable security in Scotland.

14 In perpetual rent-charges charged on land in England and Wales or Northern Ireland and fee-farm rents (not being rent-charges) issuing out of such land, *and in feu-duties or ground annuals in Scotland.*

[**15** In Certificates of Tax Deposit.]

[**16** In fixed-interest or variable interest securities issued by the government of a relevant state.

17 In any securities the payment of interest on which is guaranteed by the government of a relevant state.

18 In fixed-interest securities issued in any relevant state by any public authority or nationalised industry or undertaking in that state.

19 In fixed-interest or variable interest securities issued in a relevant state by the government of any overseas territory within the Commonwealth or by any public or local authority within such a territory.

References in this paragraph to an overseas territory or to the government of such a territory shall be construed as if they occurred in the Overseas Development and Co-operation Act 1980.

20 In fixed-interest or variable interest securities issued in a relevant state by—

(a) the African Development Bank;

(b) the Asian Development Bank;

(c) the Caribbean Development Bank;

(d) the International Finance Corporation;

(e) the International Monetary Fund;

(f) the International Bank for Reconstruction and Development;

(g) the Inter-American Development Bank;

(h) the European Atomic Energy Community;

(i) the European Bank for Reconstruction and Development;

(j) the European Economic Community;

(k) the European Investment Bank; or

(l) the European Coal and Steel Community.

21 In debentures issued in any relevant state by a company incorporated in that state.

22 In loans to any authority to which this paragraph applies secured on all or any of the revenues of the authority or on a fund into which all or any of those revenues are payable, in fixed-interest or variable interest securities issued in a relevant state by any such authority in that state for the purpose of borrowing money so secured, and in deposits with any authority to which this paragraph applies by way of temporary loan made on the giving of a receipt for the loan by the treasurer or other similar officer of the authority and on the giving of an undertaking by the authority that, if requested to charge the loan as aforesaid, it will either comply with the request or repay the loan.

This paragraph applies to the following authorities, that is to say—

(a) any local authority in a relevant state; or

(b) any authority all the members of which are appointed or elected by one or more local authorities in any such state.

23 In deposits with a mutual investment society whose head office is located in a relevant state.

24 In loans secured on any interest in property in a relevant state which corresponds to an interest in property falling within paragraph 13 of this Part of this Schedule.]

NOTES

Amendment
Repealed, except in so far as this Schedule is applied by or under any other enactment, by virtue of the Trustee Act 2000, s 40(1), (3), Sch 2, Pt I, para 1(1), Sch 4, Pt I (for transitional provisions and savings in connection with the repeal of para 14, see s 40(2) of, and Sch 3, para 7 to, the 2000 Act).
Date in force: 1 February 2001: see SI 2001/49, art 2.
Para 1: words in square brackets inserted by SI 1977/831, art 3.

Paras 4A, 5A, 9A: inserted by SI 1977/1878, art 3.
Para 5: first words in square brackets inserted by SI 1983/772, art 2(a), words in square brackets therein inserted by SI 1991/999, art 2; second words in square brackets inserted by SI 1964/1404, art 1; third words in square brackets inserted by SI 1972/1818, art 3, words in square brackets therein inserted by SI 1983/772, art 2(b).
Para 5B: inserted by SI 1983/772, art 2(c); words in square brackets inserted by SI 1991/999, art 2.
Para 7: words in square brackets inserted by SI 1966/401, art 1.
Para 8: repealed by the Agriculture and Forestry (Financial Provisions) Act 1991, s 1, Schedule, Part IV.
Para 9: sub-paras (aa), (ab) inserted by the Greater London Authority Act 1999, s 387(1), (3)(a).
Date in force (for the purposes of its application to the Greater London Authority): 8 May 2000: see SI 1999/3434, art 3.
Date in force (for remaining purposes): 3 July 2000: see SI 1999/3434, art 4.
Para 9: in sub-para (d) words omitted repealed by the Greater London Authority Act 1999, ss 387(1), (3)(b), 423, Sch 34, Pt I.
Date in force (for the purposes of its application to the Greater London Authority): 8 May 2000: see SI 1999/3434, art 3.
Date in force (for remaining purposes): 3 July 2000: see SI 2000/801, art 2(2)(c), Schedule, Pt 3.
Para 9: in sub-para (d) words in square brackets beginning with the words "a police authority" substituted by the Police and Magistrates' Courts Act 1994, s 43, Sch 4, Pt II, para 47.
Para 9: in sub-para (d) words "section 3 of the Police Act 1996" in square brackets substituted by the Police Act 1996, s 103, Sch 7, para 1(2)(a).
Para 9: sub-para (da) inserted by the Police Act 1997, s 134(1), Sch 9, para 5.
Date in force: 1 April 1998: see SI 1998/354, art 2(2)(bb).
Para 9: sub-para (f) inserted by SI 1962/658, art 1.
Para 9: sub-para (g) inserted by SI 1973/1332, art 3.
Para 9: sub-paras (h), (i) inserted by SI 1986/601, art 2.
Para 9: sub-para (h) repealed by the Education Reform Act 1988, s 237, Sch 1, Sch 13, Pt I.
Para 10: repealed by the Water Act 1989, s 190, Sch 25, para 29.
Para 10A: inserted by the Finance Act 1982, s 150.
Para 10A: substituted by SI 2001/3649, art 269(1), (2).
Date in force: 1 December 2001: see SI 2001/3649, art 1.
Para 11: repealed by the Trustee Savings Bank Act 1976, s 36(2), Sch 6.
Para 12: substituted by the Building Societies Act 1986, s 120, Sch 18, Part I, para 4(2).
Para 14: words ", and in feu-duties or ground annuals in Scotland" repealed by the Abolition of Feudal Tenure etc (Scotland) Act 2000, s 76(2), Sch 13, Pt 1.
Date in force: to be appointed: see the Abolition of Feudal Tenure etc (Scotland) Act 2000, ss 71, 77(2).
Para 15: inserted by SI 1975/1710, art 3.
Paras 16–24: inserted by SI 1994/1908, art 2(2).
Para 19: sub-paras (a), (b) and words "For this purpose—" immediately preceding them substituted by the International Development Act 2002, s 19(1), Sch 3, para 1.

Date in force: 17 June 2002: see SI 2002/1408, art 2.
See Further
See further, in relation to the application of this Part of this Schedule, with modifications, in relation to eligible debt securities: the Uncertificated Securities (Amendment) (Eligible Debt Securities) Regulations 2003, SI 2003/1633, reg 15, Sch 2, paras 2(b), 8(1), (2)(a).

Part III Wider-Range Investments

1 In any securities issued in the United Kingdom by a company incorporated in the United Kingdom, being securities registered in the United Kingdom and not being securities falling within Part II of this Schedule.

[**2** In shares in a building society within the meaning of the Building Societies Act 1986.]

[**2A** In any shares in an investment company with variable capital within the meaning of the Open-Ended Investment Companies (Investment Companies with Variable Capital) Regulations 1996.]

[**3** In any units of an authorised unit trust scheme within the meaning of the Financial Services Act 1986.]

[**4** In any securities issued in any relevant state by a company incorporated in that state or by any unincorporated body constituted under the law of that state, not being (in either case) securities falling within Part II of this Schedule or paragraph 6 of this Part of this Schedule.

5 In shares in a mutual investment society whose head office is located in a relevant state.

6 In any units of a collective investment scheme which is—

    (a)   a recognised scheme within the meaning of the Financial Services Act 1986 which is constituted in a relevant state; or

    (b)   a UCITS;
and which does not fall within Part II of this Schedule.]

NOTES

Amendment
Repealed, except in so far as this Schedule is applied by or under any other enactment, by virtue of the Trustee Act 2000, s 40(1), (3), Sch 2, Pt I, para 1(1), Sch 4, Pt I.
   Date in force: 1 February 2001: see SI 2001/49, art 2.
Para 2: substituted by the Building Societies Act 1986, s 120, Sch 18, Part I, para 4(3).
Para 2A: inserted by SI 1996/2827, reg 75, Sch 8, para 1.
   Para 2A: substituted by SI 2001/1228, reg 84, Sch 7, Pt I, para 1.
   Date in force: 1 December 2001 (being the date on which the Financial Services and Markets Act 2000, s 19, came into force): see SI 2001/3538, art 2(1) and SI 2001/1228, reg 1(2)(c).
Para 3: substituted by the Financial Services Act 1986, s 212(2), Sch 16, para 2.
   Para 3: words omitted repealed by SI 2001/3649, art 269(1), (3).
   Date in force: 1 December 2001: see SI 2001/3649, art 1.

Paras 4–6: inserted by SI 1994/1908, art 2(3).
  Para 6: substituted by SI 2001/3649, art 269(1), (4).
  Date in force: 1 December 2001: see SI 2001/3649, art 1.
See Further
See further, in relation to the application of this Part of this Schedule, with modifications, in relation to eligible debt securities: the Uncertificated Securities (Amendment) (Eligible Debt Securities) Regulations 2003, SI 2003/1633, reg 15, Sch 2, paras 2(b), 8(1), (2)(a).

Part IV Supplemental

1 The securities mentioned in Parts I to III of this Schedule do not include any securities where the holder can be required to accept repayment of the principal, or the payment of any interest, otherwise than in sterling[, in the currency of a relevant state or in the european currency unit (as defined in article 1 of Council Regulation No 3180/78/EEC)].

2 The securities mentioned in paragraphs 1 to 8 of Part II, other than Treasury Bills or Tax Reserve Certificates, securities issued before the passing of this Act by the Government of the Isle of Man, securities falling within paragraph 4 of the said Part II issued before the passing of this Act or securities falling within paragraph 9 of that Part, and the securities mentioned in paragraph 1 of Part III of this Schedule, do not include—

    (a)   securities the price of which is not quoted on [a recognised investment exchange within the meaning of the Financial Services Act 1986 [or on an investment exchange which constitutes the principal or only market established in a relevant state on which securities admitted to official listing are dealt in or traded]]

    (b)   shares or debenture stock not fully paid up (except shares or debenture stock which by the terms of issue are required to be fully paid up within nine months of the date of issue).

[**2A** The securities mentioned in paragraphs 16 to 21 of Part II of this Schedule, other than securities traded on a relevant money market or securities falling within paragraph 22 of Part II of this Schedule, and the securities mentioned in paragraph 4 of Part III of this Schedule do not include—

    (a)   securities the price for which is not quoted on a recognised investment exchange within the meaning of the Financial Services Act 1986 or on an investment exchange which constitutes the principal or only market established in a relevant state on which securities admitted to official listing are dealt in or traded;

    (b)   shares or debenture stock not fully paid up (except shares or debenture stock which by the terms of issue are required to be fully paid up within nine months of the date of issue or shares issued with no nominal value).]

3 The securities mentioned in paragraph 6 [and 21] of Part II and paragraph 1 [or 4] of Part III of this Schedule do not include—

(a)   shares or debentures of an incorporated company of which the total issued and paid up share capital is less than one million pounds;

[(ab) shares or debentures of an incorporated company of which the total issued and paid up share capital at any time on the business day before the investment is made is less than the equivalent of one million pounds in the currency of a relevant state (at the exchange rate prevailing in the United Kingdom at the close of business on the day before the investment is made);]

(b)   shares or debentures of an incorporated company which has not in each of the five years immediately preceding the calendar year in which the investment is made paid a dividend on all the shares issued by the company, excluding any shares issued after the dividend was declared and any shares which by their terms of issue did not rank for the dividend for that year.

For the purposes of sub-paragraph (b) of this paragraph a company formed—

(i)   to take over the business of another company or other companies, or

(ii) to acquire the securities of, or control of, another company or other companies,

or for either of those purposes and for other purposes shall be deemed to have paid a dividend as mentioned in that sub-paragraph in any year in which such a dividend has been paid by the other company or all the other companies, as the case may be.

[For the purposes of sub-paragraph (b) of this paragraph in relation to investment in shares or debentures of a successor company within the meaning of the Electricity (Northern Ireland) Order 1992 the company shall be deemed to have paid a dividend as mentioned in that sub-paragraph—

(iii) in every year preceding the calendar year in which the transfer date within the meaning of Part III of that Order of 1992 falls ("the first investment year") which is included in the relevant five years; and

(iv) in the first investment year, if that year is included in the relevant five years and that company does not in fact pay such a dividend in that year; and

"the relevant five years" means the five years immediately preceding the year in which the investment in question is made or proposed to be made.]

[3A

...]

4 In this Schedule, unless the context otherwise requires, the following expressions have the meanings hereby respectively assigned to them, that is to say—

"debenture" includes debenture stock and bonds, whether constituting a charge on assets or not, and loan stock or notes;

"enactment" includes an enactment of the Parliament of Northern Ireland;

"fixed-interest securities" means securities which under their terms of issue bear a fixed rate of interest;

"local authority" in relation to the United Kingdom, means any of the following authorities—

(a) in England and Wales, the council of a county, [a county borough,] a ... borough ... an urban or rural district or a parish, the Common Council of the City of London [the Greater London Council] and the Council of the Isles of Scilly;

(b) in Scotland, a local authority within the meaning of the Local Government (Scotland) Act, 1947;

(c) ...

["mutual investment society" means a credit institution which operates on mutual principles and which is authorised by the appropriate supervisory authority of a relevant state;

"relevant money market" means a money market which is supervised by the central bank, or a government agency, of a relevant state;

"relevant state" means Austria, Finland, Iceland, [Liechtenstein,] Norway, Sweden or a member state other than the United Kingdom;]

...

"securities" includes shares, debentures [units within paragraph 3 [or 6] of Part III of this Schedule], Treasury Bills and Tax Reserve Certificates;

"shares" includes stock;

"Treasury Bills" includes ... bills issued by Her Majesty's Government in the United Kingdom and Northern Ireland Treasury Bills.

5 It is hereby declared that in this Schedule "mortgage", in relation to freehold or leasehold property in Northern Ireland, includes a registered charge which, by virtue of subsection (4) of section forty of the Local Registration of Title (Ireland) Act, 1891, or any other enactment, operates as a mortgage by deed.

6 [In relation to the United Kingdom,] references in this Schedule to an incorporated company are references to a company incorporated by or under any enactment and include references to a body of persons established for the purpose of trading for profit and incorporated by Royal Charter.

[6A References in this Schedule to a UCITS are references to a collective investment scheme which is constituted in a relevant state and which complies with the conditions necessary for it to enjoy the rights conferred by Council Directive 85/611/EEC co-ordinating the laws, regulations and administrative provisions relating to undertakings for collective investment in transferable securities; and section 86(8) of the Financial Services Act 1986 (meaning of "constituted in a member state") shall apply for the purposes of this paragraph as it applies for the purposes of that section but as if for references in that section to a member state there were substituted references to a relevant state.]

7

...

NOTES

Amendment
Repealed, except in so far as this Schedule is applied by or under any other enactment, by virtue of the Trustee Act 2000, s 40(1), (3), Sch 2, Pt I, para 1(1), Sch 4, Pt I.
   Date in force: to be appointed: see the Trustee Act 2000, s 42(2).
Paras 1, 6: words in square brackets inserted by SI 1994/1908, art 3(2), (7).
   Para 2: in sub-para (a) words in square brackets beginning with the words "a recognised investment exchange" substituted by the Financial Services Act 1986, s 212(2), Sch 16, para 2.
   Para 2: in sub-para (a) words omitted repealed by SI 2001/3649, art 269(1), (5).
   Date in force: 1 December 2001: see SI 2001/3649, art 1.
   Para 2: in sub-para (a) words from "or on an" to "dealt in or traded" in square brackets inserted by SI 1994/1908, art 3(3).
   Para 2A: inserted by SI 1994/1908, art 3(4).
   Para 2A: in sub-para (a) words omitted repealed by SI 2001/3649, art 269(1), (5).
   Date in force: 1 December 2001: see SI 2001/3649, art 1.
Para 3: first and second words in square brackets and sub-para (ab) inserted by SI 1994/1908, art 3(5); final words in square brackets inserted by SI 1992/232, art 4.
Para 3A: inserted by the Housing (Consequential Provisions) Act 1985, s 4, Sch 2, para 5; repealed by the Building Societies Act 1986, s 120, Sch 19, Part I.
Para 4: in definition "local authority", in sub-para (a) first words in square brackets inserted by the Local Government (Wales) Act 1994, s 66(6), Sch 16, para 19(2), first words omitted repealed by London Government Act 1963, s 93(1), Sch 18 Part II, final words omitted repealed by the Local Government Act 1972, s 272(1), Sch 30, final words in square brackets inserted by the London Government Act 1963, s 83(1), Sch 17, sub-para (c) repealed by the Statute Law (Repeals) Act 1981; definitions "mutual investment society", "relevant money market", "relevant state" inserted by SI 1994/1908, art 3(6)(a), in definition "relevant state" word in square brackets inserted by SI 1995/768, art 2; definitions "ordinary deposits" and "special invest-ment" repealed by the Trustee Savings Banks Act 1976, s 36(2), Sch 6; in definition "securities" first words in square brackets inserted by the Financial Services Act 1986, s 212(2), Sch 16, para 2, words in square brackets therein inserted by SI 1994/1908, art 3(6)(b); in definition "Treasury Bills" words omitted repealed by the National Loans Act 1968, s 24(2), Sch 6, Part 1.
   Para 4A: inserted by SI 2001/3649, art 269(1), (6).
   Date in force: 1 December 2001: see SI 2001/3649, art 1.
   Para 6A: inserted by SI 1994/1908, art 3(8).
   Para 6A: repealed by SI 2001/3649, art 269(1), (7).
   Date in force: 1 December 2001: see SI 2001/3649, art 1.
Para 7: repealed by the Building Societies Act 1986, s 120, Sch 19, Part I.

SCHEDULE 2 (SECTION 3)
MODIFICATION OF S 2 IN RELATION TO PROPERTY FALLING
WITHIN S 3(3)

1 In this Schedule "special-range property" means property falling within subsection (3) of section three of this Act.

2 (1) Where a trust fund includes special-range property, subsection (1) of section two of this Act shall have effect as if references to the trust fund were references to so much thereof as does not consist of special-range property, and the special-range property shall be carried to a separate part of the fund.

(2) Any property which—

(a) being property belonging to the narrower-range or wider-range part of a trust fund, is converted into special-range property, or

(b) being special-range property, accrues to a trust fund after the division of the fund or part thereof in pursuance of subsection (1) of section two of this Act or of that subsection as modified by sub-paragraph (1) of this paragraph,

shall be carried to such a separate part of the fund as aforesaid; and subsections (2) and (3) of the said section two shall have effect subject to this sub-paragraph.

3 Where property carried to such a separate part as aforesaid is converted into property other than special-range property,—

(a) it shall be transferred to the narrower-range part of the fund or the wider-range part of the fund or apportioned between them, and

(b) any transfer of property from one of those parts to the other shall be made which is necessary to secure that the value of each of those parts of the fund is increased by the same amount.

NOTES

Amendment
Repealed, except in so far as this section relates to a trustee having a power of investment conferred on him under any enactment which was passed before 3 August 1961 and which is not amended by the Trustee Act 2000, Sch 2, by the Trustee Act 2000, s 40(1), (3), Sch 2, Pt I, para 1(2), Sch 4, Pt I.
Date in force: 1 February 2001: see SI 2001/49, art 2.

SCHEDULE 3 (SECTION 3)
PROVISIONS SUPPLEMENTARY TO S 3(4)

1 Where in a case falling within subsection (4) of section three of this Act, property belonging to the narrower-range part of a trust fund—

(a) is invested otherwise than in a narrower-range investment, or

(b) being so invested, is retained and not transferred or as soon as may be reinvested as mentioned in subsection (2) of section two of this Act, then, so long as the property continues so invested and comprised in the narrower-range part of the fund, section one of this Act shall not authorise the making or retention of any wider-range investment.

2 Section four of the Trustee Act 1925, or section thirty-three of the Trusts (Scotland) Act, 1921 (which relieve a trustee from liability for retaining an investment which has ceased to be authorised), shall not apply where an investment ceased to be authorised in consequence of the foregoing paragraph.

NOTES

Amendment
Repealed, except in so far as this section relates to a trustee having a power of investment conferred on him under any enactment which was passed before 3 August 1961 and which is not amended by the Trustee Act 2000, Sch 2, by the Trustee Act 2000, s 40(1), (3), Sch 2, Pt I, para 1(2), Sch 4, Pt I.
  Date in force: 1 February 2001: see SI 2001/49, art 2.

SCHEDULE 4 (SECTION 16)
MINOR AND CONSEQUENTIAL AMENDMENTS

1 (1) ...

(2) References in the Trusts (Scotland) Act 1921, to section ten or eleven of that Act, or to provisions which include either of those sections, shall be construed respectively as references to section one of this Act and as including references to that section.

2–6

< ... >

NOTES

Amendment
Para 1: sub-para (1) repealed by the Trustee Act 2000, s 40(1), (3), Sch 2, Pt I, para 1(3)(b), Sch 4, Pt I.
  Date in force: 1 February 2001: see SI 2001/49, art 2.
Para 2: repealed by the Building Societies Act 1962, s 131, Sch 10, Part I.
Paras 4, 5: repealed by the National Savings Bank Act 1971, s 28, Sch 2.
Para 6: repealed by the Housing (Consequential Provisions) Act 1985, s 3, Sch 1, Part I.

App 2.2

Trusts of Land and Appointment of Trustees Act 1996, ss 1, 6, 7, 8, 10, 11, 12, 13, 14 and 15

Part I Trusts of Land

Introductory

1 Meaning of "trust of land"

(1) In this Act—

    (a)   "trust of land" means (subject to subsection (3)) any trust of property which consists of or includes land, and

    (b)   "trustees of land" means trustees of a trust of land.

(2) The reference in subsection (1)(a) to a trust—

    (a)   is to any description of trust (whether express, implied, resulting or constructive), including a trust for sale and a bare trust, and

    (b)   includes a trust created, or arising, before the commencement of this Act.

(3) The reference to land in subsection (1)(a) does not include land which (despite section 2) is settled land or which is land to which the Universities and College Estates Act 1925 applies.

Functions of trustees of land

6 General powers of trustees

(1) For the purpose of exercising their functions as trustees, the trustees of land have in relation to the land subject to the trust all the powers of an absolute owner.

(2) Where in the case of any land subject to a trust of land each of the beneficiaries interested in the land is a person of full age and capacity who is absolutely entitled to the land, the powers conferred on the trustees by subsection (1) include the power to convey the land to the beneficiaries even though they have not required the trustees to do so; and where land is conveyed by virtue of this subsection—

    (a)   the beneficiaries shall do whatever is necessary to secure that it vests in them, and

    (b)   if they fail to do so, the court may make an order requiring them to do so.

(3) The trustees of land have power to [acquire land under the power conferred by section 8 of the Trustee Act 2000].

(4) ...

(5) In exercising the powers conferred by this section trustees shall have regard to the rights of the beneficiaries.

(6) The powers conferred by this section shall not be exercised in contravention of, or of any order made in pursuance of, any other enactment or any rule of law or equity.

(7) The reference in subsection (6) to an order includes an order of any court or of the Charity Commissioners.

(8) Where any enactment other than this section confers on trustees authority to act subject to any restriction, limitation or condition, trustees of land may not exercise the powers conferred by this section to do any act which they are prevented from doing under the other enactment by reason of the restriction, limitation or condition.

[(9) The duty of care under section 1 of the Trustee Act 2000 applies to trustees of land when exercising the powers conferred by this section.]

NOTES

Amendment
Sub-s (3): words "acquire land under the power conferred by section 8 of the Trustee Act 2000" in square brackets substituted by the Trustee Act 2000, s 40(1), Sch 2, Pt II, para 45(1).
   Date in force: 1 February 2001: see SI 2001/49, art 2.
   Sub-s (4): repealed by the Trustee Act 2000, s 40(1), (3), Sch 2, Pt II, para 45(2), Sch 4, Pt II.
   Date in force: 1 February 2001: see SI 2001/49, art 2.
   Sub-s (9): inserted by the Trustee Act 2000, s 40(1), Sch 2, Pt II, para 45(3).
   Date in force: 1 February 2001: see SI 2001/49, art 2.

7 Partition by trustees

(1) The trustees of land may, where beneficiaries of full age are absolutely entitled in undivided shares to land subject to the trust, partition the land, or any part of it, and provide (by way of mortgage or otherwise) for the payment of any equality money.

(2) The trustees shall give effect to any such partition by conveying the partitioned land in severalty (whether or not subject to any legal mortgage created for raising equality money), either absolutely or in trust, in accordance with the rights of those beneficiaries.

(3) Before exercising their powers under subsection (2) the trustees shall obtain the consent of each of those beneficiaries.

(4) Where a share in the land is affected by an incumbrance, the trustees may either give effect to it or provide for its discharge from the property allotted to that share as they think fit.

(5) If a share in the land is absolutely vested in a minor, subsections (1) to (4) apply as if he were of full age, except that the trustees may act on his behalf and retain land or other property representing his share in trust for him.

8   Exclusion and restriction of powers

(1) Sections 6 and 7 do not apply in the case of a trust of land created by a disposition in so far as provision to the effect that they do not apply is made by the disposition.

(2) If the disposition creating such a trust makes provision requiring any consent to be obtained to the exercise of any power conferred by section 6 or 7, the power may not be exercised without that consent.

(3) Subsection (1) does not apply in the case of charitable, ecclesiastical or public trusts.

(4) Subsections (1) and (2) have effect subject to any enactment which prohibits or restricts the effect of provision of the description mentioned in them.

[ss 9 and 9A omitted]

Consents and consultation

10   Consents

(1) If a disposition creating a trust of land requires the consent of more than two persons to the exercise by the trustees of any function relating to the land, the consent of any two of them to the exercise of the function is sufficient in favour of a purchaser.

(2) Subsection (1) does not apply to the exercise of a function by trustees of land held on charitable, ecclesiastical or public trusts.

(3) Where at any time a person whose consent is expressed by a disposition creating a trust of land to be required to the exercise by the trustees of any function relating to the land is not of full age—

   (a)   his consent is not, in favour of a purchaser, required to the exercise of the function, but

   (b)   the trustees shall obtain the consent of a parent who has parental responsibility for him (within the meaning of the Children Act 1989) or of a guardian of his.

11   Consultation with beneficiaries

(1) The trustees of land shall in the exercise of any function relating to land subject to the trust—

(a)   so far as practicable, consult the beneficiaries of full age and beneficially entitled to an interest in possession in the land, and

(b)   so far as consistent with the general interest of the trust, give effect to the wishes of those beneficiaries, or (in case of dispute) of the majority (according to the value of their combined interests).

(2) Subsection (1) does not apply—

(a)   in relation to a trust created by a disposition in so far as provision that it does not apply is made by the disposition,

(b)   in relation to a trust created or arising under a will made before the commencement of this Act, or

(c)   in relation to the exercise of the power mentioned in section 6(2).

(3) Subsection (1) does not apply to a trust created before the commencement of this Act by a disposition, or a trust created after that commencement by reference to such a trust, unless provision to the effect that it is to apply is made by a deed executed—

(a)   in a case in which the trust was created by one person and he is of full capacity, by that person, or

(b)   in a case in which the trust was created by more than one person, by such of the persons who created the trust as are alive and of full capacity.

(4) A deed executed for the purposes of subsection (3) is irrevocable.

Right of beneficiaries to occupy trust land

12   The right to occupy

(1) A beneficiary who is beneficially entitled to an interest in possession in land subject to a trust of land is entitled by reason of his interest to occupy the land at any time if at that time—

(a)   the purposes of the trust include making the land available for his occupation (or for the occupation of beneficiaries of a class of which he is a member or of beneficiaries in general), or

(b)   the land is held by the trustees so as to be so available.

(2) Subsection (1) does not confer on a beneficiary a right to occupy land if it is either unavailable or unsuitable for occupation by him.

(3) This section is subject to section 13.

13   Exclusion and restriction of right to occupy

(1) Where two or more beneficiaries are (or apart from this subsection would be) entitled under section 12 to occupy land, the trustees of land may exclude or restrict the entitlement of any one or more (but not all) of them.

(2) Trustees may not under subsection (1)—

    (a)   unreasonably exclude any beneficiary's entitlement to occupy land, or

    (b)   restrict any such entitlement to an unreasonable extent.

(3) The trustees of land may from time to time impose reasonable conditions on any beneficiary in relation to his occupation of land by reason of his entitlement under section 12.

(4) The matters to which trustees are to have regard in exercising the powers conferred by this section include—

    (a)   the intentions of the person or persons (if any) who created the trust,

    (b)   the purposes for which the land is held, and

    (c)   the circumstances and wishes of each of the beneficiaries who is (or apart from any previous exercise by the trustees of those powers would be) entitled to occupy the land under section 12.

(5) The conditions which may be imposed on a beneficiary under subsection (3) include, in particular, conditions requiring him—

    (a)   to pay any outgoings or expenses in respect of the land, or

    (b)   to assume any other obligation in relation to the land or to any activity which is or is proposed to be conducted there.

(6) Where the entitlement of any beneficiary to occupy land under section 12 has been excluded or restricted, the conditions which may be imposed on any other beneficiary under subsection (3) include, in particular, conditions requiring him to—

    (a)   make payments by way of compensation to the beneficiary whose entitlement has been excluded or restricted, or

    (b)   forgo any payment or other benefit to which he would otherwise be entitled under the trust so as to benefit that beneficiary.

(7) The powers conferred on trustees by this section may not be exercised—

    (a)   so as prevent any person who is in occupation of land (whether or not by reason of an entitlement under section 12) from continuing to occupy the land, or

    (b)   in a manner likely to result in any such person ceasing to occupy the land,

unless he consents or the court has given approval.

(8) The matters to which the court is to have regard in determining whether to give approval under subsection (7) include the matters mentioned in subsection (4)(a) to (c).

Powers of court

14   Applications for order

(1) Any person who is a trustee of land or has an interest in a property subject to a trust of land may make an application to the court for an order under this section.

(2) On an application for an order under this section the court may make any such order—

> (a)   relating to the exercise by the trustees of any of their functions (including an order relieving them of any obligation to obtain the consent of, or to consult, any person in connection with the exercise of any of their functions), or

> (b)   declaring the nature or extent of a person's interest in property subject to the trust,

as the court thinks fit.

(3) The court may not under this section make any order as to the appointment or removal of trustees.

(4) The powers conferred on the court by this section are exercisable on an application whether it is made before or after the commencement of this Act.

15   Matters relevant in determining applications

(1) The matters to which the court is to have regard in determining an application for an order under section 14 include—

> (a)   the intentions of the person or persons (if any) who created the trust,

> (b)   the purposes for which the property subject to the trust is held,

> (c)   the welfare of any minor who occupies or might reasonably be expected to occupy any land subject to the trust as his home, and

> (d)   the interests of any secured creditor of any beneficiary.

(2) In the case of an application relating to the exercise in relation to any land of the powers conferred on the trustees by section 13, the matters to which the court is to have regard also include the circumstances and wishes of each of the beneficiaries who is (or apart from any previous exercise by the trustees of those powers would be) entitled to occupy the land under section 12.

(3) In the case of any other application, other than one relating to the exercise of the power mentioned in section 6(2), the matters to which the court is to have regard also include the circumstances and wishes of any beneficiaries of full age and entitled to an interest in possession in property subject to the trust or (in case of dispute) of the majority (according to the value of their combined interests).

(4) This section does not apply to an application if section 335A of the Insolvency Act 1986 (which is inserted by Schedule 3 and relates to applications by a trustee of a bankrupt) applies to it.

App 2.3

Trustee Act 2000

Part I The Duty of Care

1 The duty of care

(1) Whenever the duty under this subsection applies to a trustee, he must exercise such care and skill as is reasonable in the circumstances, having regard in particular—

    (a)   to any special knowledge or experience that he has or holds himself out as having, and

    (b)   if he acts as trustee in the course of a business or profession, to any special knowledge or experience that it is reasonable to expect of a person acting in the course of that kind of business or profession.

(2) In this Act the duty under subsection (1) is called "the duty of care".

2 Application of duty of care

Schedule 1 makes provision about when the duty of care applies to a trustee.

Part II Investment

3 General power of investment

(1) Subject to the provisions of this Part, a trustee may make any kind of investment that he could make if he were absolutely entitled to the assets of the trust.

(2) In this Act the power under subsection (1) is called "the general power of investment".

(3) The general power of investment does not permit a trustee to make investments in land other than in loans secured on land (but see also section 8).

(4) A person invests in a loan secured on land if he has rights under any contract under which—

    (a)   one person provides another with credit, and

(b)   the obligation of the borrower to repay is secured on land.

(5) "Credit" includes any cash loan or other financial accommodation.

(6) "Cash" includes money in any form.

4   Standard investment criteria

(1) In exercising any power of investment, whether arising under this Part or otherwise, a trustee must have regard to the standard investment criteria.

(2) A trustee must from time to time review the investments of the trust and consider whether, having regard to the standard investment criteria, they should be varied.

(3) The standard investment criteria, in relation to a trust, are—

(a)   the suitability to the trust of investments of the same kind as any particular investment proposed to be made or retained and of that particular investment as an investment of that kind, and

(b)   the need for diversification of investments of the trust, in so far as is appropriate to the circumstances of the trust.

5   Advice

(1) Before exercising any power of investment, whether arising under this Part or otherwise, a trustee must (unless the exception applies) obtain and consider proper advice about the way in which, having regard to the standard investment criteria, the power should be exercised.

(2) When reviewing the investments of the trust, a trustee must (unless the exception applies) obtain and consider proper advice about whether, having regard to the standard investment criteria, the investments should be varied.

(3) The exception is that a trustee need not obtain such advice if he reasonably concludes that in all the circumstances it is unnecessary or inappropriate to do so.

(4) Proper advice is the advice of a person who is reasonably believed by the trustee to be qualified to give it by his ability in and practical experience of financial and other matters relating to the proposed investment.

6   Restriction or exclusion of this Part etc

(1) The general power of investment is—

(a)   in addition to powers conferred on trustees otherwise than by this Act, but

(b)   subject to any restriction or exclusion imposed by the trust instrument or by any enactment or any provision of subordinate legislation.

(2) For the purposes of this Act, an enactment or a provision of subordinate legislation is not to be regarded as being, or as being part of, a trust instrument.

(3) In this Act "subordinate legislation" has the same meaning as in the Interpretation Act 1978.

7   Existing trusts

(1) This Part applies in relation to trusts whether created before or after its commencement.

(2) No provision relating to the powers of a trustee contained in a trust instrument made before 3rd August 1961 is to be treated (for the purposes of section 6(1)(b)) as restricting or excluding the general power of investment.

(3) A provision contained in a trust instrument made before the commencement of this Part which—

(a)   has effect under section 3(2) of the Trustee Investments Act 1961 as a power to invest under that Act, or

(b)   confers power to invest under that Act,
is to be treated as conferring the general power of investment on a trustee.

Part III Acquisition of Land

8   Power to acquire freehold and leasehold land

(1) A trustee may acquire freehold or leasehold land in the United Kingdom—

(a)   as an investment,

(b)   for occupation by a beneficiary, or

(c)   for any other reason.

(2) "Freehold or leasehold land" means—

(a)   in relation to England and Wales, a legal estate in land,

(b)   in relation to Scotland—

(i)   the estate or interest of the proprietor of the dominium utile or, in the case of land not held on feudal tenure, the estate or interest of the owner, or

(ii) a tenancy, and

(c) in relation to Northern Ireland, a legal estate in land, including land held under a fee farm grant.

(3) For the purpose of exercising his functions as a trustee, a trustee who acquires land under this section has all the powers of an absolute owner in relation to the land.

9 Restriction or exclusion of this Part etc

The powers conferred by this Part are—

(a) in addition to powers conferred on trustees otherwise than by this Part, but

(b) subject to any restriction or exclusion imposed by the trust instrument or by any enactment or any provision of subordinate legislation.

10 Existing trusts

(1) This Part does not apply in relation to—

(a) a trust of property which consists of or includes land which (despite section 2 of the Trusts of Land and Appointment of Trustees Act 1996) is settled land, or

(b) a trust to which the Universities and College Estates Act 1925 applies.

(2) Subject to subsection (1), this Part applies in relation to trusts whether created before or after its commencement.

Part IV Agents, nominees and custodians

Agents

11 Power to employ agents

(1) Subject to the provisions of this Part, the trustees of a trust may authorise any person to exercise any or all of their delegable functions as their agent.

(2) In the case of a trust other than a charitable trust, the trustees' delegable functions consist of any function other than—

(a) any function relating to whether or in what way any assets of the trust should be distributed,

(b)   any power to decide whether any fees or other payment due to be made out of the trust funds should be made out of income or capital,

(c)   any power to appoint a person to be a trustee of the trust, or

(d)   any power conferred by any other enactment or the trust instrument which permits the trustees to delegate any of their functions or to appoint a person to act as a nominee or custodian.

(3) In the case of a charitable trust, the trustees' delegable functions are—

(a)   any function consisting of carrying out a decision that the trustees have taken;

(b)   any function relating to the investment of assets subject to the trust (including, in the case of land held as an investment, managing the land and creating or disposing of an interest in the land);

(c)   any function relating to the raising of funds for the trust otherwise than by means of profits of a trade which is an integral part of carrying out the trust's charitable purpose;

(d)   any other function prescribed by an order made by the Secretary of State.

(4) For the purposes of subsection (3)(c) a trade is an integral part of carrying out a trust's charitable purpose if, whether carried on in the United Kingdom or elsewhere, the profits are applied solely to the purposes of the trust and either—

(a)   the trade is exercised in the course of the actual carrying out of a primary purpose of the trust, or

(b)   the work in connection with the trade is mainly carried out by beneficiaries of the trust.

(5) The power to make an order under subsection (3)(d) is exercisable by statutory instrument which shall be subject to annulment in pursuance of a resolution of either House of Parliament.

12   Persons who may act as agents

(1) Subject to subsection (2), the persons whom the trustees may under section 11 authorise to exercise functions as their agent include one or more of their number.

(2) The trustees may not authorise two (or more) persons to exercise the same function unless they are to exercise the function jointly.

(3) The trustees may not under section 11 authorise a beneficiary to exercise any function as their agent (even if the beneficiary is also a trustee).

(4) The trustees may under section 11 authorise a person to exercise functions as their agent even though he is also appointed to act as their nominee or custodian (whether under section 16, 17 or 18 or any other power).

13 Linked functions etc

(1) Subject to subsections (2) and (5), a person who is authorised under section 11 to exercise a function is (whatever the terms of the agency) subject to any specific duties or restrictions attached to the function.

For example, a person who is authorised under section 11 to exercise the general power of investment is subject to the duties under section 4 in relation to that power.

(2) A person who is authorised under section 11 to exercise a power which is subject to a requirement to obtain advice is not subject to the requirement if he is the kind of person from whom it would have been proper for the trustees, in compliance with the requirement, to obtain advice.

(3) Subsections (4) and (5) apply to a trust to which section 11(1) of the Trusts of Land and Appointment of Trustees Act 1996 (duties to consult beneficiaries and give effect to their wishes) applies.

(4) The trustees may not under section 11 authorise a person to exercise any of their functions on terms that prevent them from complying with section 11(1) of the 1996 Act.

(5) A person who is authorised under section 11 to exercise any function relating to land subject to the trust is not subject to section 11(1) of the 1996 Act.

14 Terms of agency

(1) Subject to subsection (2) and sections 15(2) and 29 to 32, the trustees may authorise a person to exercise functions as their agent on such terms as to remuneration and other matters as they may determine.

(2) The trustees may not authorise a person to exercise functions as their agent on any of the terms mentioned in subsection (3) unless it is reasonably necessary for them to do so.

(3) The terms are—

    (a)   a term permitting the agent to appoint a substitute;

    (b)   a term restricting the liability of the agent or his substitute to the trustees or any beneficiary;

    (c)   a term permitting the agent to act in circumstances capable of giving rise to a conflict of interest.

15   Asset management: special restrictions

(1) The trustees may not authorise a person to exercise any of their asset management functions as their agent except by an agreement which is in or evidenced in writing.

(2) The trustees may not authorise a person to exercise any of their asset management functions as their agent unless—

   (a)   they have prepared a statement that gives guidance as to how the functions should be exercised ("a policy statement"), and

   (b)   the agreement under which the agent is to act includes a term to the effect that he will secure compliance with—

      (i)   the policy statement, or

      (ii)   if the policy statement is revised or replaced under section 22, the revised or replacement policy statement.

(3) The trustees must formulate any guidance given in the policy statement with a view to ensuring that the functions will be exercised in the best interests of the trust.

(4) The policy statement must be in or evidenced in writing.

(5) The asset management functions of trustees are their functions relating to—

   (a)   the investment of assets subject to the trust,

   (b)   the acquisition of property which is to be subject to the trust, and

   (c)   managing property which is subject to the trust and disposing of, or creating or disposing of an interest in, such property.

Nominees and custodians

16   Power to appoint nominees

(1) Subject to the provisions of this Part, the trustees of a trust may—

   (a)   appoint a person to act as their nominee in relation to such of the assets of the trust as they determine (other than settled land), and

   (b)   take such steps as are necessary to secure that those assets are vested in a person so appointed.

(2) An appointment under this section must be in or evidenced in writing.

(3) This section does not apply to any trust having a custodian trustee or in relation to any assets vested in the official custodian for charities.

17 Power to appoint custodians

(1) Subject to the provisions of this Part, the trustees of a trust may appoint a person to act as a custodian in relation to such of the assets of the trust as they may determine.

(2) For the purposes of this Act a person is a custodian in relation to assets if he undertakes the safe custody of the assets or of any documents or records concerning the assets.

(3) An appointment under this section must be in or evidenced in writing.

(4) This section does not apply to any trust having a custodian trustee or in relation to any assets vested in the official custodian for charities.

18 Investment in bearer securities

(1) If trustees retain or invest in securities payable to bearer, they must appoint a person to act as a custodian of the securities.

(2) Subsection (1) does not apply if the trust instrument or any enactment or provision of subordinate legislation contains provision which (however expressed) permits the trustees to retain or invest in securities payable to bearer without appointing a person to act as a custodian.

(3) An appointment under this section must be in or evidenced in writing.

(4) This section does not apply to any trust having a custodian trustee or in relation to any securities vested in the official custodian for charities.

19 Persons who may be appointed as nominees or custodians

(1) A person may not be appointed under section 16, 17 or 18 as a nominee or custodian unless one of the relevant conditions is satisfied.

(2) The relevant conditions are that—

    (a)   the person carries on a business which consists of or includes acting as a nominee or custodian;

    (b)   the person is a body corporate which is controlled by the trustees;

    (c)   the person is a body corporate recognised under section 9 of the Administration of Justice Act 1985.

(3) The question whether a body corporate is controlled by trustees is to be determined in accordance with section 840 of the Income and Corporation Taxes Act 1988.

(4) The trustees of a charitable trust which is not an exempt charity must act in accordance with any guidance given by the Charity Commissioners concerning the selection of a person for appointment as a nominee or custodian under section 16, 17 or 18.

(5) Subject to subsections (1) and (4), the persons whom the trustees may under section 16, 17 or 18 appoint as a nominee or custodian include—

  (a)   one of their number, if that one is a trust corporation, or

  (b)   two (or more) of their number, if they are to act as joint nominees or joint custodians.

(6) The trustees may under section 16 appoint a person to act as their nominee even though he is also—

  (a)   appointed to act as their custodian (whether under section 17 or 18 or any other power), or

  (b)   authorised to exercise functions as their agent (whether under section 11 or any other power).

(7) Likewise, the trustees may under section 17 or 18 appoint a person to act as their custodian even though he is also—

  (a)   appointed to act as their nominee (whether under section 16 or any other power), or

  (b)   authorised to exercise functions as their agent (whether under section 11 or any other power).

20   Terms of appointment of nominees and custodians

(1) Subject to subsection (2) and sections 29 to 32, the trustees may under section 16, 17 or 18 appoint a person to act as a nominee or custodian on such terms as to remuneration and other matters as they may determine.

(2) The trustees may not under section 16, 17 or 18 appoint a person to act as a nominee or custodian on any of the terms mentioned in subsection (3) unless it is reasonably necessary for them to do so.

(3) The terms are—

  (a)   a term permitting the nominee or custodian to appoint a substitute;

  (b)   a term restricting the liability of the nominee or custodian or his substitute to the trustees or to any beneficiary;

  (c)   a term permitting the nominee or custodian to act in circumstances capable of giving rise to a conflict of interest.

Review of and liability for agents, nominees and custodians etc

21   Application of sections 22 and 23

(1) Sections 22 and 23 apply in a case where trustees have, under section 11, 16, 17 or 18—

(a)   authorised a person to exercise functions as their agent, or

(b)   appointed a person to act as a nominee or custodian.

(2) Subject to subsection (3), sections 22 and 23 also apply in a case where trustees have, under any power conferred on them by the trust instrument or by any enactment or any provision of subordinate legislation—

(a)   authorised a person to exercise functions as their agent, or

(b)   appointed a person to act as a nominee or custodian.

(3) If the application of section 22 or 23 is inconsistent with the terms of the trust instrument or the enactment or provision of subordinate legislation, the section in question does not apply.

22   Review of agents, nominees and custodians etc

(1) While the agent, nominee or custodian continues to act for the trust, the trustees—

(a)   must keep under review the arrangements under which the agent, nominee or custodian acts and how those arrangements are being put into effect,

(b)   if circumstances make it appropriate to do so, must consider whether there is a need to exercise any power of intervention that they have, and

(c)   if they consider that there is a need to exercise such a power, must do so.

(2) If the agent has been authorised to exercise asset management functions, the duty under subsection (1) includes, in particular—

(a)   a duty to consider whether there is any need to revise or replace the policy statement made for the purposes of section 15,

(b)   if they consider that there is a need to revise or replace the policy statement, a duty to do so, and

(c)   a duty to assess whether the policy statement (as it has effect for the time being) is being complied with.

(3) Subsections (3) and (4) of section 15 apply to the revision or replacement of a policy statement under this section as they apply to the making of a policy statement under that section.

(4) "Power of intervention" includes—

(a)   a power to give directions to the agent, nominee or custodian;

(b)   a power to revoke the authorisation or appointment.

23 Liability for agents, nominees and custodians etc

(1) A trustee is not liable for any act or default of the agent, nominee or custodian unless he has failed to comply with the duty of care applicable to him, under paragraph 3 of Schedule 1—

    (a)   when entering into the arrangements under which the person acts as agent, nominee or custodian, or

    (b)   when carrying out his duties under section 22.

(2) If a trustee has agreed a term under which the agent, nominee or custodian is permitted to appoint a substitute, the trustee is not liable for any act or default of the substitute unless he has failed to comply with the duty of care applicable to him, under paragraph 3 of Schedule 1—

    (a)   when agreeing that term, or

    (b)   when carrying out his duties under section 22 in so far as they relate to the use of the substitute.

Supplementary

24 Effect of trustees exceeding their powers

A failure by the trustees to act within the limits of the powers conferred by this Part—

    (a)   in authorising a person to exercise a function of theirs as an agent, or

    (b)   in appointing a person to act as a nominee or custodian,
does not invalidate the authorisation or appointment.

25 Sole trustees

(1) Subject to subsection (2), this Part applies in relation to a trust having a sole trustee as it applies in relation to other trusts (and references in this Part to trustees—except in sections 12(1) and (3) and 19(5)—are to be read accordingly).

(2) Section 18 does not impose a duty on a sole trustee if that trustee is a trust corporation.

26 Restriction or exclusion of this Part etc

The powers conferred by this Part are—

    (a)   in addition to powers conferred on trustees otherwise than by this Act, but

(b)   subject to any restriction or exclusion imposed by the trust instrument or by any enactment or any provision of subordinate legislation.

27   Existing trusts

This Part applies in relation to trusts whether created before or after its commencement.

Part V Remuneration

28   Trustee's entitlement to payment under trust instrument

(1) Except to the extent (if any) to which the trust instrument makes inconsistent provision, subsections (2) to (4) apply to a trustee if—

(a)   there is a provision in the trust instrument entitling him to receive payment out of trust funds in respect of services provided by him to or on behalf of the trust, and

(b)   the trustee is a trust corporation or is acting in a professional capacity.

(2) The trustee is to be treated as entitled under the trust instrument to receive payment in respect of services even if they are services which are capable of being provided by a lay trustee.

(3) Subsection (2) applies to a trustee of a charitable trust who is not a trust corporation only—

(a)   if he is not a sole trustee, and

(b)   to the extent that a majority of the other trustees have agreed that it should apply to him.

(4) Any payments to which the trustee is entitled in respect of services are to be treated as remuneration for services (and not as a gift) for the purposes of—

(a)   section 15 of the Wills Act 1837 (gifts to an attesting witness to be void), and

(b)   section 34(3) of the Administration of Estates Act 1925 (order in which estate to be paid out).

(5) For the purposes of this Part, a trustee acts in a professional capacity if he acts in the course of a profession or business which consists of or includes the provision of services in connection with—

(a) the management or administration of trusts generally or a particular kind of trust, or

(b) any particular aspect of the management or administration of trusts generally or a particular kind of trust,

and the services he provides to or on behalf of the trust fall within that description.

(6) For the purposes of this Part, a person acts as a lay trustee if he—

(a) is not a trust corporation, and

(b) does not act in a professional capacity.

29 Remuneration of certain trustees

(1) Subject to subsection (5), a trustee who—

(a) is a trust corporation, but

(b) is not a trustee of a charitable trust,

is entitled to receive reasonable remuneration out of the trust funds for any services that the trust corporation provides to or on behalf of the trust.

(2) Subject to subsection (5), a trustee who—

(a) acts in a professional capacity, but

(b) is not a trust corporation, a trustee of a charitable trust or a sole trustee,

is entitled to receive reasonable remuneration out of the trust funds for any services that he provides to or on behalf of the trust if each other trustee has agreed in writing that he may be remunerated for the services.

(3) "Reasonable remuneration" means, in relation to the provision of services by a trustee, such remuneration as is reasonable in the circumstances for the provision of those services to or on behalf of that trust by that trustee and for the purposes of subsection (1) includes, in relation to the provision of services by a trustee who is an authorised institution under the Banking Act 1987 and provides the services in that capacity, the institution's reasonable charges for the provision of such services.

(4) A trustee is entitled to remuneration under this section even if the services in question are capable of being provided by a lay trustee.

(5) A trustee is not entitled to remuneration under this section if any provision about his entitlement to remuneration has been made—

(a) by the trust instrument, or

(b) by any enactment or any provision of subordinate legislation.

(6) This section applies to a trustee who has been authorised under a power conferred by Part IV or the trust instrument—

(a) to exercise functions as an agent of the trustees, or

(b) to act as a nominee or custodian,

as it applies to any other trustee.

30 Remuneration of trustees of charitable trusts

(1) The Secretary of State may by regulations make provision for the remuneration of trustees of charitable trusts who are trust corporations or act in a professional capacity.

(2) The power under subsection (1) includes power to make provision for the remuneration of a trustee who has been authorised under a power conferred by Part IV or any other enactment or any provision of subordinate legislation, or by the trust instrument—

(a) to exercise functions as an agent of the trustees, or

(b) to act as a nominee or custodian.

(3) Regulations under this section may—

(a) make different provision for different cases;

(b) contain such supplemental, incidental, consequential and transitional provision as the Secretary of State considers appropriate.

(4) The power to make regulations under this section is exercisable by statutory instrument, but no such instrument shall be made unless a draft of it has been laid before Parliament and approved by a resolution of each House of Parliament.

31 Trustees' expenses

(1) A trustee—

(a) is entitled to be reimbursed from the trust funds, or

(b) may pay out of the trust funds,

expenses properly incurred by him when acting on behalf of the trust.

(2) This section applies to a trustee who has been authorised under a power conferred by Part IV or any other enactment or any provision of subordinate legislation, or by the trust instrument—

(a) to exercise functions as an agent of the trustees, or

(b) to act as a nominee or custodian,

as it applies to any other trustee.

32 Remuneration and expenses of agents, nominees and custodians

(1) This section applies if, under a power conferred by Part IV or any other enactment or any provision of subordinate legislation, or by the trust instrument, a person other than a trustee has been—

    (a)   authorised to exercise functions as an agent of the trustees, or

    (b)   appointed to act as a nominee or custodian.

(2) The trustees may remunerate the agent, nominee or custodian out of the trust funds for services if—

    (a)   he is engaged on terms entitling him to be remunerated for those services, and

    (b)   the amount does not exceed such remuneration as is reasonable in the circumstances for the provision of those services by him to or on behalf of that trust.

(3) The trustees may reimburse the agent, nominee or custodian out of the trust funds for any expenses properly incurred by him in exercising functions as an agent, nominee or custodian.

33 Application

(1) Subject to subsection (2), sections 28, 29, 31 and 32 apply in relation to services provided to or on behalf of, or (as the case may be) expenses incurred on or after their commencement on behalf of, trusts whenever created.

(2) Nothing in section 28 or 29 is to be treated as affecting the operation of—

    (a)   section 15 of the Wills Act 1837, or

    (b)   section 34(3) of the Administration of Estates Act 1925,
in relation to any death occurring before the commencement of section 28 or (as the case may be) section 29.

Part VI Miscellaneous and Supplementary

34 Power to insure

(1) For section 19 of the Trustee Act 1925 (power to insure) substitute—

19 Power to insure

(1) A trustee may—

(a) insure any property which is subject to the trust against risks of loss or damage due to any event, and

(b) pay the premiums out of the trust funds.

(2) In the case of property held on a bare trust, the power to insure is subject to any direction given by the beneficiary or each of the beneficiaries—

(a) that any property specified in the direction is not to be insured;

(b) that any property specified in the direction is not to be insured except on such conditions as may be so specified.

(3) Property is held on a bare trust if it is held on trust for—

(a) a beneficiary who is of full age and capacity and absolutely entitled to the property subject to the trust, or

(b) beneficiaries each of whom is of full age and capacity and who (taken together) are absolutely entitled to the property subject to the trust.

(4) If a direction under subsection (2) of this section is given, the power to insure, so far as it is subject to the direction, ceases to be a delegable function for the purposes of section 11 of the Trustee Act 2000 (power to employ agents).

(5) In this section "trust funds" means any income or capital funds of the trust."

(2) In section 20(1) of the Trustee Act 1925 (application of insurance money) omit "whether by fire or otherwise".

(3) The amendments made by this section apply in relation to trusts whether created before or after its commencement.

35 Personal representatives

(1) Subject to the following provisions of this section, this Act applies in relation to a personal representative administering an estate according to the law as it applies to a trustee carrying out a trust for beneficiaries.

(2) For this purpose this Act is to be read with the appropriate modifications and in particular—

(a) references to the trust instrument are to be read as references to the will,

(b) references to a beneficiary or to beneficiaries, apart from the reference to a beneficiary in section 8(1)(b), are to be read as references to a person or the persons interested in the due administration of the estate, and

(c) the reference to a beneficiary in section 8(1)(b) is to be read as a reference to a person who under the will of the deceased or under the law relating to intestacy is beneficially interested in the estate.

(3) Remuneration to which a personal representative is entitled under section 28 or 29 is to be treated as an administration expense for the purposes of—

(a)   section 34(3) of the Administration of Estates Act 1925 (order in which estate to be paid out), and

(b)   any provision giving reasonable administration expenses priority over the preferential debts listed in Schedule 6 to the Insolvency Act 1986.

(4) Nothing in subsection (3) is to be treated as affecting the operation of the provisions mentioned in paragraphs (a) and (b) of that subsection in relation to any death occurring before the commencement of this section.

36   Pension schemes

(1) In this section "pension scheme" means an occupational pension scheme (within the meaning of the Pension Schemes Act 1993) established under a trust and subject to the law of England and Wales.

(2) Part I does not apply in so far as it imposes a duty of care in relation to—

(a)   the functions described in paragraphs 1 and 2 of Schedule 1, or

(b)   the functions described in paragraph 3 of that Schedule to the extent that they relate to trustees—

(i)   authorising a person to exercise their functions with respect to investment, or

(ii)   appointing a person to act as their nominee or custodian.

(3) Nothing in Part II or III applies to the trustees of any pension scheme.

(4) Part IV applies to the trustees of a pension scheme subject to the restrictions in subsections (5) to (8).

(5) The trustees of a pension scheme may not under Part IV authorise any person to exercise any functions relating to investment as their agent.

(6) The trustees of a pension scheme may not under Part IV authorise a person who is—

(a)   an employer in relation to the scheme, or

(b)   connected with or an associate of such an employer,
to exercise any of their functions as their agent.

(7) For the purposes of subsection (6)—

(a)   "employer", in relation to a scheme, has the same meaning as in the Pensions Act 1995;

    (b)   sections 249 and 435 of the Insolvency Act 1986 apply for the purpose of determining whether a person is connected with or an associate of an employer.

(8) Sections 16 to 20 (powers to appoint nominees and custodians) do not apply to the trustees of a pension scheme.

37   Authorised unit trusts

(1) Parts II to IV do not apply to trustees of authorised unit trusts.

(2) "Authorised unit trust" means a unit trust scheme in the case of which an order under section 78 of the Financial Services Act 1986 is in force.

38   Common investment schemes for charities etc

Parts II to IV do not apply to—

    (a)   trustees managing a fund under a common investment scheme made, or having effect as if made, under section 24 of the Charities Act 1993, other than such a fund the trusts of which provide that property is not to be transferred to the fund except by or on behalf of a charity the trustees of which are the trustees appointed to manage the fund, or

    (b)   trustees managing a fund under a common deposit scheme made, or having effect as if made, under section 25 of that Act.

39   Interpretation

(1) In this Act—

"asset" includes any right or interest;

"charitable trust" means a trust under which property is held for charitable purposes and "charitable purposes" has the same meaning as in the Charities Act 1993;

"custodian trustee" has the same meaning as in the Public Trustee Act 1906;

"enactment" includes any provision of a Measure of the Church Assembly or of the General Synod of the Church of England;

"exempt charity" has the same meaning as in the Charities Act 1993;

"functions" includes powers and duties;

"legal mortgage" has the same meaning as in the Law of Property Act 1925;

"personal representative" has the same meaning as in the Trustee Act 1925;

"settled land" has the same meaning as in the Settled Land Act 1925;

"trust corporation" has the same meaning as in the Trustee Act 1925;

"trust funds" means income or capital funds of the trust.

(2) In this Act the expressions listed below are defined or otherwise explained by the provisions indicated—

asset management functions	section 15(5)
custodian	section 17(2)
the duty of care	section 1(2)
the general power of investment	section 3(2)
lay trustee	section 28(6)
power of intervention	section 22(4)
the standard investment criteria	section 4(3)
subordinate legislation	section 6(3)
trustee acting in a professional capacity	section 28(5)
trust instrument	sections 6(2) and 35(2)(a)

40 Minor and consequential amendments etc

(1) Schedule 2 (minor and consequential amendments) shall have effect.

(2) Schedule 3 (transitional provisions and savings) shall have effect.

(3) Schedule 4 (repeals) shall have effect.

41 Power to amend other Acts

(1) A Minister of the Crown may by order make such amendments of any Act, including an Act extending to places outside England and Wales, as appear to him appropriate in consequence of or in connection with Part II or III.

(2) Before exercising the power under subsection (1) in relation to a local, personal or private Act, the Minister must consult any person who appears to him to be affected by any proposed amendment.

(3) An order under this section may—

(a) contain such transitional provisions and savings as the Minister thinks fit;

(b) make different provision for different purposes.

(4) The power to make an order under this section is exercisable by statutory instrument which shall be subject to annulment in pursuance of a resolution of either House of Parliament.

(5) "Minister of the Crown" has the same meaning as in the Ministers of the Crown Act 1975.

42   Commencement and extent

(1) Section 41, this section and section 43 shall come into force on the day on which this Act is passed.

(2) The remaining provisions of this Act shall come into force on such day as the Lord Chancellor may appoint by order made by statutory instrument; and different days may be so appointed for different purposes.

(3) An order under subsection (2) may contain such transitional provisions and savings as the Lord Chancellor considers appropriate in connection with the order.

(4) Subject to section 41(1) and subsection (5), this Act extends to England and Wales only.

(5) An amendment or repeal in Part II or III of Schedule 2 or Part II of Schedule 4 has the same extent as the provision amended or repealed.

43   Short title

This Act may be cited as the Trustee Act 2000.

SCHEDULE 1 (SECTION 2)
APPLICATION OF DUTY OF CARE

Investment

1 The duty of care applies to a trustee—

    (a)   when exercising the general power of investment or any other power of investment, however conferred;

    (b)   when carrying out a duty to which he is subject under section 4 or 5 (duties relating to the exercise of a power of investment or to the review of investments).

Acquisition of land

2 The duty of care applies to a trustee—

    (a)   when exercising the power under section 8 to acquire land;

    (b)   when exercising any other power to acquire land, however conferred;

(c)   when exercising any power in relation to land acquired under a power mentioned in sub-paragraph (a) or (b).

Agents, nominees and custodians

3 (1) The duty of care applies to a trustee—

(a)   when entering into arrangements under which a person is author-ised under section 11 to exercise functions as an agent;

(b)   when entering into arrangements under which a person is appointed under section 16 to act as a nominee;

(c)   when entering into arrangements under which a person is appointed under section 17 or 18 to act as a custodian;

(d)   when entering into arrangements under which, under any other power, however conferred, a person is authorised to exercise functions as an agent or is appointed to act as a nominee or custodian;

(e)   when carrying out his duties under section 22 (review of agent, nominee or custodian, etc).

(2) For the purposes of sub-paragraph (1), entering into arrangements under which a person is authorised to exercise functions or is appointed to act as a nominee or custodian includes, in particular—

(a)   selecting the person who is to act,

(b)   determining any terms on which he is to act, and

(c)   if the person is being authorised to exercise asset management functions, the preparation of a policy statement under section 15.

Compounding of liabilities

4 The duty of care applies to a trustee—

(a)   when exercising the power under section 15 of the Trustee Act 1925 to do any of the things referred to in that section;

(b)   when exercising any corresponding power, however conferred.

Insurance

5 The duty of care applies to a trustee—

(a)   when exercising the power under section 19 of the Trustee Act 1925 to insure property;

(b)   when exercising any corresponding power, however conferred.

Reversionary interests, valuations and audit

6 The duty of care applies to a trustee—

(a) when exercising the power under section 22(1) or (3) of the Trustee Act 1925 to do any of the things referred to there;

(b) when exercising any corresponding power, however conferred.

Exclusion of duty of care

7 The duty of care does not apply if or in so far as it appears from the trust instrument that the duty is not meant to apply.

SCHEDULE 2 (SECTION 40)
MINOR AND CONSEQUENTIAL AMENDMENTS

Part I The Trustee Investments Act 1961 and the Charities Act 1993

The Trustee Investments Act 1961 (c 62)

1 (1) Sections 1, 2, 5, 6, 12, 13 and 15 shall cease to have effect, except in so far as they are applied by or under any other enactment.

(2) Section 3 and Schedules 2 and 3 shall cease to have effect, except in so far as they relate to a trustee having a power of investment conferred on him under an enactment—

(a) which was passed before the passing of the 1961 Act, and

(b) which is not amended by this Schedule.

(3) Omit—

(a) sections 8 and 9,

(b) paragraph 1(1) of Schedule 4, and

(c) section 16(1), in so far as it relates to paragraph 1(1) of Schedule 4.

The Charities Act 1993 (c 10)

2 (1) Omit sections 70 and 71.

(2) In section 86(2) in paragraph (a)—

(a) omit "70", and

(b) at the end insert "or".

(3) Omit section 86(2)(b).

Part II Other Public General Acts

The Places of Worship Sites Act 1873 (c 50)

3 In section 2 (payment of purchase money, etc) for "shall be invested upon such securities or investments as would for the time being be authorised by statute or the Court of Chancery" substitute "shall be invested under the general power of investment in section 3 of the Trustee Act 2000".

The Technical and Industrial Institutions Act 1892 (c 29)

4 In section 9 (investment powers relating to proceeds of sale of land acquired under the Act) for subsection (5) substitute—

"(5) Money arising by sale may, until reinvested in the purchase of land, be invested—

(a)   in the names of the governing body, in any investments in which trustees may invest under the general power of investment in section 3 of the Trustee Act 2000 (as restricted by sections 4 and 5 of that Act), or

(b)   under the general power of investment in section 3 of that Act, by trustees for the governing body or by a person authorised by the trustees under that Act to invest as an agent of the trustees.

(6) Any profits from investments under subsection (5) shall be invested in the same way and added to capital until the capital is reinvested in the purchase of land."

The Duchy of Cornwall Management Act 1893 (c 20)

5 The 1893 Act is hereby repealed.

The Duchy of Lancaster Act 1920 (c 51)

6 In section 1 (extension of powers of investment of funds of Duchy of Lancaster) for "in any of the investments specified in paragraph (a) of section one of the Trustees Act 1893 and any enactment amending or extending that paragraph" substitute "under the general power of investment in section 3 of the Trustee Act 2000 (as restricted by sections 4 and 5 of that Act)".

The Settled Land Act 1925 (c 18)

7 In section 21 (absolute owners subject to certain interests to have the powers of tenant for life), in subsection (1)(d) for "income thereof" substitute "resultant profits".

8 In section 39 (regulations respecting sales), in subsection (2), in the proviso, for the words from "accumulate" to the end of the subsection substitute "accumulate the profits from the capital money by investing them and any resulting profits under the general power of investment in section 3 of the Trustee Act 2000 and shall add the accumulations to capital."

9 In section 73 (modes of investment or application), in subsection (1) for paragraph (i) substitute—

> "(i) In investment in securities either under the general power of investment in section 3 of the Trustee Act 2000 or under a power to invest conferred on the trustees of the settlement by the settlement;".

10 (1) In section 75 (regulations respecting investment, devolution, and income of securities etc), for subsection (2) substitute—

"(2) Subject to Part IV of the Trustee Act 2000, to section 75A of this Act and to the following provisions of this section—

> (a) the investment or other application by the trustees shall be made according to the discretion of the trustees, but subject to any consent required or direction given by the settlement with respect to the investment or other application by the trustees of trust money of the settlement, and
>
> (b) any investment shall be in the names or under the control of the trustees."

(2) For subsection (4) of that section substitute—

"(4) The trustees, in exercising their power to invest or apply capital money, shall—

> (a) so far as practicable, consult the tenant for life; and
>
> (b) so far as consistent with the general interest of the settlement, give effect to his wishes.

(4A) Any investment or other application of capital money under the direction of the court shall not during the subsistence of the beneficial interest of the tenant for life be altered without his consent.

(4B) The trustees may not under section 11 of the Trustee Act 2000 authorise a person to exercise their functions with respect to the investment or application of capital money on terms that prevent them from complying with subsection (4) of this section.

(4C) A person who is authorised under section 11 of the Trustee Act 2000 to exercise any of their functions with respect to the investment or application of capital money is not subject to subsection (4) of this section."

(3) Nothing in this paragraph affects the operation of section 75 in relation to directions of the tenant for life given, but not acted upon by the trustees, before the commencement of this paragraph.

11 After section 75 insert—

"75A   Power to accept charge as security for part payment for land sold

(1) Where—

    (a)   land subject to the settlement is sold by the tenant for life or statutory owner, for an estate in fee simple or a term having at least five hundred years to run, and

    (b)   the proceeds of sale are liable to be invested,

the tenant for life or statutory owner may, with the consent of the trustees of the settlement, contract that the payment of any part, not exceeding two-thirds, of the purchase money shall be secured by a charge by way of legal mortgage of the land sold, with or without the security of any other property.

(2) If any buildings are comprised in the property secured by the charge, the charge must contain a covenant by the mortgagor to keep them insured for their full value against loss or damage due to any event.

(3) A person exercising the power under subsection (1) of this section, or giving consent for the purposes of that subsection—

    (a)   is not required to comply with section 5 of the Trustee Act 2000 before giving his consent, and

    (b)   is not liable for any loss incurred merely because the security is insufficient at the date of the charge.

(4) The power under subsection (1) of this section is exercisable subject to the consent of any person whose consent to a change of investment is required by the instrument, if any, creating the trust.

(5) Where the sale referred to in subsection (1) of this section is made under the order of the court, the power under that subsection applies only if and as far as the court may by order direct."

12 Omit section 96 (protection of each trustee individually).

13 In section 98 (protection of trustees in particular cases), omit subsections (1) and (2).

14 Omit section 100 (trustees' reimbursements).

15 In section 102 (management of land during minority or pending contingency), in subsection (2) for paragraph (e) substitute—

    "(e)   to insure against risks of loss or damage due to any event under section 19 of the Trustee Act 1925;".

16 (1) In section 104 (powers of tenant for life not assignable etc)—

    (a)   in subsection (3)(b) omit "authorised by statute for the investment of trust money", and

    (b)   in subsection (4)(b) for the words from "no investment" to "trust money;" substitute "the consent of the assignee shall be required to an investment of capital money for the time being affected by the assignment in investments other than securities, and to any application of such capital money;".

(2) Sub-paragraph (1) applies to the determination on or after the commencement of that sub-paragraph of whether an assignee's consent is required to the investment or application of capital money.

17 In section 107 (tenant for life deemed to be in the position and to have the duties and liabilities of a trustee, etc) after subsection (1) insert—

"(1A) The following provisions apply to the tenant for life as they apply to the trustees of the settlement—

    (a)   sections 11, 13 to 15 and 21 to 23 of the Trustee Act 2000 (power to employ agents subject to certain restrictions),

    (b)   section 32 of that Act (remuneration and expenses of agents etc),

    (c)   section 19 of the Trustee Act 1925 (power to insure), and

    (d)   in so far as they relate to the provisions mentioned in paragraphs (a) and (c), Part I of, and Schedule 1 to, the Trustee Act 2000 (the duty of care)."

The Trustee Act 1925 (c 19)

18 Omit Part I (investments).

19 In section 14 (power of trustees to give receipts) in subsection (1) after "securities," insert "investments".

20 In section 15 (power to compound liabilities), for "in good faith" substitute "if he has or they have discharged the duty of care set out in section 1(1) of the Trustee Act 2000".

21 Omit section 21 (deposit of documents for safe custody).

22 In section 22 (reversionary interests, valuations, and audit)—

    (a)   in subsection (1), for "in good faith" substitute "if they have discharged the duty of care set out in section 1(1) of the Trustee Act 2000", and

    (b)   in subsection (3), omit "in good faith" and at the end insert "if the trustees have discharged the duty of care set out in section 1(1) of the Trustee Act 2000".

23 Omit section 23 (power to employ agents).

24 Omit section 30 (implied indemnity of trustees).

25 In section 31(2) (power to invest income during minority) for "in the way of compound interest by investing the same and the resulting income thereof" substitute "by investing it, and any profits from so investing it".

The Land Registration Act 1925 (c 21)

26 In section 94(1) (registered land subject to a trust to be registered in the names of the trustees), at the end insert "or in the name of a nominee appointed under section 16 of the Trustee Act 2000".

The Administration of Estates Act 1925 (c 23)

27 In section 33, in subsection (3) (investment during minority of beneficiary or the subsistence of a life interest) for the words from "in any investments for the time being authorised by statute" to the end of the subsection substitute "under the Trustee Act 2000."

28 In section 39 (powers of management) after subsection (1) insert—

"(1A) Subsection (1) of this section is without prejudice to the powers conferred on personal representatives by the Trustee Act 2000."

The Universities and College Estates Act 1925 (c 24)

29 In section 26 (modes of application of capital money) in subsection (1) for paragraph (i) substitute—

"(i) In investments in which trustees may invest under the general power of investment in section 3 of the Trustee Act 2000 (as restricted by sections 4 and 5 of that Act);".

The Regimental Charitable Funds Act 1935 (c 11)

30 In section 2(1) (application of funds held on account of regimental charitable funds)—

(a) in paragraph (a) for "in some manner" to "trusts" substitute "under the general power of investment in section 3 of the Trustee Act 2000";

(b) in paragraph (b) after "the income" insert "or the other profits".

The Agricultural Marketing Act 1958 (c 47)

31 (1) In section 16 (investment of surplus funds of boards) for paragraph (a) substitute—

"(a) the moneys of the board not for the time being required by them for the purposes of their functions are not, except with the approval of the Minister, invested otherwise than in investments in which trustees may invest under the general power of investment in section 3 of the Trustee Act 2000 (as restricted by sections 4 and 5 of that Act); and".

(2) Any scheme made under the 1958 Act and in effect before the day on which sub-paragraph (1) comes into force shall be treated, in relation to the

making of investments on and after that day, as including provision permitting investment by the board in accordance with section 16(a) of the 1958 Act as amended by sub-paragraph (1).

The Horticulture Act 1960 (c 22)

32 In section 13 (miscellaneous financial powers of organisations promoting home-grown produce) for subsection (3) substitute—

"(3) A relevant organisation may invest any of its surplus money which is not for the time being required for any other purpose in any investments in which trustees may invest under the general power of investment in section 3 of the Trustee Act 2000 (as restricted by sections 4 and 5 of that Act)".

The House of Commons Members' Fund Act 1962 (c 53)

33 (1) In section 1 (powers of investment of trustees of House of Commons Members' Fund)—

    (a)   in subsection (2) omit "Subject to the following provisions of this section";

    (b)   omit subsections (3) to (5).

(2) In section 2 (interpretation etc) omit subsection (1).

The Betting, Gaming and Lotteries Act 1963 (c 2)

34 In section 25(1) (general powers and duties of the Horserace Betting Levy Board) for paragraph (e) substitute—

    "(e) to make such other investments as—

        (i)   they judge desirable for the proper conduct of their affairs, and

        (ii)   a trustee would be able to make under the general power of investment in section 3 of the Trustee Act 2000 (as restricted by sections 4 and 5 of that Act);".

The Cereals Marketing Act 1965 (c 14)

35 (1) In section 18, in subsection (2) (Home-Grown Cereals Authority's power to invest reserve funds) for "in accordance with the next following subsection" substitute "in any investments in which trustees may invest under the general power of investment in section 3 of the Trustee Act 2000 (as restricted by sections 4 and 5 of that Act)."

(2) Omit section 18(3).

The Agriculture Act 1967 (c 22)

36 (1) In section 18, in subsection (2) (Meat and Livestock Commission's power to invest reserve fund) for "in accordance with the next following subsection" substitute "in any investments in which trustees may invest under the general power of investment in section 3 of the Trustee Act 2000 (as restricted by sections 4 and 5 of that Act)."

(2) Omit section 18(3).

The Solicitors Act 1974 (c 47)

37 In Schedule 2, for paragraph 3 (power of Law Society to invest) substitute—

"3 The Society may invest any money which forms part of the fund in any investments in which trustees may invest under the general power of investment in section 3 of the Trustee Act 2000 (as restricted by sections 4 and 5 of that Act)."

The Policyholders Protection Act 1975 (c 75)

38 In Schedule 1, in paragraph 7, for sub-paragraph (1) (power of Policyholders Protection Board to invest) substitute—

"(1) The Board may invest any funds held by them which appear to them to be surplus to their requirements for the time being—

    (a)   in any investments in which trustees may invest under the general power of investment in section 3 of the Trustee Act 2000 (as restricted by sections 4 and 5 of that Act); or

    (b)   in any investment approved for the purpose by the Treasury."

The National Heritage Act 1980 (c 17)

39 In section 6 for subsection (3) (powers of investment of Trustees of National Heritage Memorial Fund) substitute—

"(3) The Trustees may invest any sums to which subsection (2) does not apply in any investments in which trustees may invest under the general power of investment in section 3 of the Trustee Act 2000 (as restricted by sections 4 and 5 of that Act)."

The Licensing (Alcohol Education and Research) Act 1981 (c 28)

40 In section 7 (powers of investment of Alcohol Education and Research Council) for subsection (5) substitute—

"(5) Any sums in the Fund which are not immediately required for any other purpose may be invested by the Council in any investments in which trustees may invest under the general power of investment in section 3 of the Trustee Act 2000 (as restricted by sections 4 and 5 of that Act)."

The Fisheries Act 1981 (c 29)

41 For section 10 (powers of investment of Sea Fish Industry Authority) substitute—

10 "Investment of reserve funds

Any money of the Authority which is not immediately required for any other purpose may be invested by the Authority in any investments in which trustees may invest under the general power of investment in section 3 of the Trustee Act 2000 (as restricted by sections 4 and 5 of that Act)".

The Duchy of Cornwall Management Act 1982 (c 47)

42 For section 1 (powers of investment of Duchy property) substitute—

1 "Powers of investment of Duchy property

The power of investment conferred by the Duchy of Cornwall Management Act 1863 includes power to invest in any investments in which trustees may invest under the general power of investment in section 3 of the Trustee Act 2000 (as restricted by sections 4 and 5 of that Act)."

43 In—

    (a)   section 6(3) (Duchy of Cornwall Management Acts extended in relation to banking), and

    (b)   section 11(2) (collective citation of Duchy of Cornwall Management Acts),

for "Duchy of Cornwall Management Acts 1868 to 1893" substitute "Duchy of Cornwall Management Acts 1863 to 1868".

The Administration of Justice Act 1982 (c 53)

44 In section 42 (common investment schemes) in subsection (6) for paragraph (a) substitute—

    "(a)   he may invest trust money in shares in the fund without obtaining and considering advice on whether to make such an investment; and".

The Trusts of Land and Appointment of Trustees Act 1996 (c 47)

45 (1) In section 6 (general powers of trustees), in subsection (3) for "purchase a legal estate in any land in England and Wales" substitute "acquire land under the power conferred by section 8 of the Trustee Act 2000."

(2) Omit subsection (4) of that section.

(3) After subsection (8) of that section insert—

"(9) The duty of care under section 1 of the Trustee Act 2000 applies to trustees of land when exercising the powers conferred by this section."

46 In section 9 (delegation by trustees) omit subsection (8).

47 After section 9 insert—

"9A   Duties of trustees in connection with delegation etc

(1) The duty of care under section 1 of the Trustee Act 2000 applies to trustees of land in deciding whether to delegate any of their functions under section 9.

(2) Subsection (3) applies if the trustees of land—

    (a)   delegate any of their functions under section 9, and

    (b)   the delegation is not irrevocable.

(3) While the delegation continues, the trustees—

    (a)   must keep the delegation under review,

    (b)   if circumstances make it appropriate to do so, must consider whether there is a need to exercise any power of intervention that they have, and

    (c)   if they consider that there is a need to exercise such a power, must do so.

(4) "Power of intervention" includes—

    (a)   a power to give directions to the beneficiary;

    (b)   a power to revoke the delegation.

(5) The duty of care under section 1 of the 2000 Act applies to trustees in carrying out any duty under subsection (3).

(6) A trustee of land is not liable for any act or default of the beneficiary, or beneficiaries, unless the trustee fails to comply with the duty of care in deciding to delegate any of the trustees' functions under section 9 or in carrying out any duty under subsection (3).

(7) Neither this section nor the repeal of section 9(8) by the Trustee Act 2000 affects the operation after the commencement of this section of any delegation effected before that commencement."

48 Omit section 17(1) (application of section 6(3) in relation to trustees of proceeds of sale of land).

49 In Schedule 3 (consequential amendments) omit paragraph 3(4) (amendment of section 19(1) and (2) of Trustee Act 1925).

Part III Measures

The Ecclesiastical Dilapidations Measure 1923 (No 3)

50 In section 52, in subsection (5) (investment of sums held in relation to repair of chancels)—

    (a)   for "in any investment permitted by law for the investment of trust funds, and the yearly income resulting therefrom shall be applied," substitute "in any investments in which trustees may invest under the general power of investment in section 3 of the Trustee Act 2000, and the annual profits from the investments shall be applied"; and

    (b)   in paragraph (iii) for "any residue of the said income not applied as aforesaid in any year" substitute "any residue of the profits from the investments not applied in any year."

The Diocesan Stipends Funds Measure 1953 (No 2)

51 In section 4 (application of moneys credited to capital accounts) in subsection (1) for paragraph (bc) substitute—

"(bc) investment in any investments in which trustees may invest under the general power of investment in section 3 of the Trustee Act 2000 (as restricted by sections 4 and 5 of that Act);".

The Church Funds Investment Measure 1958 (No 1)

52 In the Schedule, in paragraph 21 (range of investments of deposit fund) for paragraphs (a) to (d) of sub-paragraph (1) substitute—

"(aa) In any investments in which trustees may invest under the general power of investment in section 3 of the Trustee Act 2000 (as restricted by sections 4 and 5 of that Act);".

The Clergy Pensions Measure 1961 (No 3)

53 (1) In section 32 (investment powers of Board), in subsection (1), for paragraph (a) substitute—

"(a)   in any investments in which trustees may invest under the general power of investment in section 3 of the Trustee Act 2000 (as restricted by sections 4 and 5 of that Act);".

(2) Omit subsection (3) of that section.

The Repair of Benefice Buildings Measure 1972 (No 2)

54 In section 17, in subsection (2) (diocesan parsonages fund's power of investment), for "who shall have the same powers of investment as trustees of trust funds:" substitute "who shall have the same power as trustees to invest in any investments in which trustees may invest under the general power of investment in section 3 of the Trustee Act 2000 (as restricted by sections 4 and 5 of that Act)."

The Pastoral Measure 1983 (No 1)

55 In section 44, for subsection (6) (Redundant Churches Fund's power of investment) substitute—

"(6) The powers to invest any such sums are—

(a) power to invest in investments in which trustees may invest under the general power of investment in section 3 of the Trustee Act 2000 (as restricted by sections 4 and 5 of that Act); and

(b) power to invest in the investments referred to in paragraph 21(1)(e) and (f) of the Schedule to the Church Funds Investment Measure 1958."

The Church of England (Pensions) Measure 1988 (No 4)

56 Omit section 14(b) (amendment of section 32(3) of the Clergy Pensions Measure 1961).

The Cathedrals Measure 1999 (No 1)

57 In section 16 (cathedral moneys: investment powers, etc), in subsection (1)—

(a) for paragraph (c) substitute—

"(c) power to invest in any investments in which trustees may invest under the general power of investment in section 3 of the Trustee Act 2000 (as restricted by sections 4 and 5 of that Act),", and

(b) omit the words from "and the powers" to the end of the subsection.

SCHEDULE 3 (SECTION 40)
TRANSITIONAL PROVISIONS AND SAVINGS

The Trustee Act 1925 (c 19)

1 (1) Sub-paragraph (2) applies if, immediately before the day on which Part IV of this Act comes into force, a banker or banking company holds any bearer securities deposited with him under section 7(1) of the 1925 Act (investment in bearer securities).

(2) On and after the day on which Part IV comes into force, the banker or banking company shall be treated as if he had been appointed as custodian of the securities under section 18.

2 The repeal of section 8 of the 1925 Act (loans and investments by trustees not chargeable as breaches of trust) does not affect the operation of that section in relation to loans or investments made before the coming into force of that repeal.

3 The repeal of section 9 of the 1925 Act (liability for loss by reason of improper investment) does not affect the operation of that section in relation to any advance of trust money made before the coming into force of that repeal.

4 (1) Sub-paragraph (2) applies if, immediately before the day on which Part IV of this Act comes into force, a banker or banking company holds any documents deposited with him under section 21 of the 1925 Act (deposit of documents for safe custody).

(2) On and after the day on which Part IV comes into force, the banker or banking company shall be treated as if he had been appointed as custodian of the documents under section 17.

5 (1) Sub-paragraph (2) applies if, immediately before the day on which Part IV of this Act comes into force, a person has been appointed to act as or be an agent or attorney under section 23(1) or (3) of the 1925 Act (general power to employ agents etc).

(2) On and after the day on which Part IV comes into force, the agent shall be treated as if he had been authorised to exercise functions as an agent under section 11 (and, if appropriate, as if he had also been appointed under that Part to act as a custodian or nominee).

6 The repeal of section 23(2) of the 1925 Act (power to employ agents in respect of property outside the United Kingdom) does not affect the operation after the commencement of the repeal of an appointment made before that commencement.

The Trustee Investments Act 1961 (c 62)

7 (1) A trustee shall not be liable for breach of trust merely because he continues to hold an investment acquired by virtue of paragraph 14 of Part II of Schedule 1 to the 1961 Act (perpetual rent-charges etc).

(2) A person who—

    (a)   is not a trustee,

    (b)   before the commencement of Part II of this Act had powers to invest in the investments described in paragraph 14 of Part II of Schedule 1 to the 1961 Act, and

    (c)   on that commencement acquired the general power of investment, shall not be treated as exceeding his powers of investment merely because he continues to hold an investment acquired by virtue of that paragraph.

The Cathedrals Measure 1963 (No 2)

8 While section 21 of the Cathedrals Measure 1963 (investment powers, etc of capitular bodies) continues to apply in relation to any cathedral, that section shall have effect as if—

> (a)   in subsection (1), for paragraph (c) and the words from "and the powers" to the end of the subsection there were substituted—
>
> "(c)   power to invest in any investments in which trustees may invest under the general power of investment in section 3 of the Trustee Act 2000 (as restricted by sections 4 and 5 of that Act).", and
>
> (b)   in subsection (5), for "subsections (2) and (3) of section six of the Trustee Investments Act 1961" there were substituted "section 5 of the Trustee Act 2000".

SCHEDULE 4 (SECTION 40)
REPEALS

Part I The Trustee Investments Act 1961 and the Charities Act 1993

Chapter	Short title	Extent of repeal
1961 c 62.	The Trustee Investments Act 1961.	Sections 1 to 3, 5, 6, 8, 9, 12, 13, 15 and 16(1). Schedules 2 and 3. In Schedule 4, paragraph 1(1).
1993 c 10.	The Charities Act 1993.	Sections 70 and 71. In section 86(2) in paragraph (a), "70" and paragraph (b).

Note: the repeals in this Part of this Schedule have effect in accordance with Part I of Schedule 2.

Part II Other repeals

Chapter	Short title	Extent of repeal
1893 c 20.	The Duchy of Cornwall Management Act 1893.	The whole Act.

Chapter	Short title	Extent of repeal
1925 c 18.	The Settled Land Act 1925.	Section 96.
		Section 98(1) and (2).
		Section 100.
		In section 104(3)(b) the words "authorised by statute for the investment of trust money".
1925 c 19.	The Trustee Act 1925.	Part I.
		In section 20(1) the words "whether by fire or otherwise".
		Sections 21, 23 and 30.
1961 No 3.	The Clergy Pensions Measure 1961.	Section 32(3).
1962 c 53.	The House of Commons Members' Fund Act 1962.	In section 1, in subsection (2) the words "Subject to the following provisions of this section" and subsections (3) to (5).
		Section 2(1).
1965 c 14.	The Cereals Marketing Act 1965.	Section 18(3).
1967 c 22.	The Agriculture Act 1967.	Section 18(3).
1988 No 4.	The Church of England (Pensions) Measure 1988.	Section 14(b).
1996 c 47.	The Trusts of Land and Appointment of Trustees Act 1996.	Section 6(4).
		Section 9(8).
		Section 17(1).
		In Schedule 3, paragraph 3(4).
1999 No 1.	The Cathedrals Measure 1999.	In section 16(1), the words from "and the powers" to the end of the subsection.

Index